A STUDY GUIDE TO
A Separate Peace
JOHN KNOWLES

HOLT, RINEHART AND WINSTON
Harcourt Brace & Company
Austin · New York · Orlando · Atlanta · San Francisco · Boston · Dallas · Toronto · London

Writer: Donna Reardon

Copyright © by Holt, Rinehart and Winston, Inc.

Printed in the United States of America

ISBN 0-03-023444-1

89   085   9 8 7 6 5

CONTENTS

Focusing on Background   1
  The Life and Work of John Knowles
    (1926–)   1
  The Critical Response to the Novel   1
  The Source of the Story   3
Elements of the Novel   4
  The Themes of *A Separate Peace*   4
  The Setting   4
  Point of View   5
  Style   5
  The Characters   5
  Symbolism   6
  Foreshadowing   6
Teaching the Novel   7
  Introducing the Novel/Pacing the Assignment   7
  Motivating and Aiding Student Reading   7
Vocabulary from the Novel   9
Plot Synopsis and Literary Focus   12
Reading Guide Questions   19
Writing About the Novel   25
Going Beyond the Novel   26
Testing on the Novel   29
  Developing Vocabulary A   29
  Developing Vocabulary B   30
  Developing Vocabulary C   31
  Understanding What Happened/
    Recognizing Elements of the Novel   33
  Critical Thinking and Writing   35
Answer Key   36
For Further Reading   46

Introduction

Holt, Rinehart and Winston's *Elements of the Novel* Study Guides are designed to accompany the ***Elements of Literature*** Pupil's and Teacher's Editions, offering both you and your students a rich fund of information for understanding, interpreting, and appreciating a variety of novels commonly taught in seventh through twelfth-grade classrooms but not included in the ***Elements of Literature*** anthologies. Each *Elements of the Novel* Study Guide is designed to be a valuable tool for both teachers and students. Teachers, whether they are intimately familiar with the novel being covered or have never before taught—perhaps even never before read—the novel, will find that the Study Guide is an informative, time-saving resource. Students will find that the material contained in each Study Guide greatly enriches their experience of the novel by providing the same interesting, high-quality background information and questioning strategies that they have come to expect from their ***Elements of Literature*** Pupil's Edition. The Study Guide aids students' literal comprehension of their reading, deepens their interpretations of the author's meaning, increases their recognition of and facility with literary elements, stimulates their creative response to literature, and exercises their critical thinking and writing abilities.

Each *Elements of the Novel* Study Guide is designed to provide maximum versatility and flexibility to allow you to teach the novel in the way that seems best for your students and most comfortable for you. Most sections of the Study Guide are blackline masters designed to be duplicated and passed out to your students, either as the entire class reads a novel together or as individual students or small groups study a particular novel on their own. Though suggestions and teaching guidance are offered, in the end it is you, the teacher, who must decide which materials in the Study Guide to share with students, in what manner, and in what order, according to the needs and preference of the particular class. The materials in the Study Guide are not intended to lead to one prescribed interpretation of the novel, but to act as a catalyst for discussions, analyses, interpretations, conclusions, and further research.

Following is a description of the eleven major sections in the Study Guide, with suggested uses for and approaches to each.

Focusing on Background   Because an essential part of fully appreciating any novel in a critical sense is a knowledge of relevant background information, this section supplies important information about the author's life and work, the critical response to the novel, and other facts that may be brought to bear on an interpretation and appreciation of the novel: its historical context, the author's philosophical orientation, the particular genre to which the novel belongs, and so on. All or any part of this material may be duplicated and handed out to students or provided by you via lectures and discussions. Some subsections in *Focusing on Background* may be particularly helpful to students before they begin to read the novel; other subsections, such as those dealing with the critical response to the novel or the author's philosophy, may be more profit-ably shared with the students after an initial reading of the novel has been completed.

Elements of the Novel   In order to provide a focused, unified, and purposeful approach to each novel, the Study Guide presents an overview of the salient literary elements of the novel being studied. The material in this section will be valuable to you as a quick introduction to and understanding of the elements at work in the novel. Some of the material in this section may be useful for students to know before they read the novel, but you must decide which information to share and which to withhold. Study Guides containing a list of the major characters in the novel with a brief description of each could be helpful to students as they read; on the other hand, information about such elements as theme, foreshadowing, and irony, if presented too early, may deny students their own valid personal responses to their reading and rob them of any original interpretations, analyses, and conclusions about the work. It is a decided danger that, if students are told beforehand what a work is ''about,'' what it ''means,'' they will mindlessly accept these conclusions rather than exercise their critical thinking abilities to arrive at their own analyses and interpretations.

It is a good idea to review with your students the definitions of the salient literary elements in the novel they are about to study. For a quick review of literary elements, refer students to the *Handbook of Literary Terms* in the back of the ***Elements of Literature*** Pupil's Edition.

Teaching the Novel   This section provides suggestions that will help you to effectively teach the novel. It offers pragmatic advice about how long the novel might take to teach, how to introduce the novel, how to pace the assignments, and how best to use the material presented in the Study Guide. Also included in this section are ideas for motivating and aiding student reading, suggestions for using journals or Reading Logs, examples of discussion questions that might serve as good prereading strategies, and approaches for helping students to deal with particular difficulties the novel may present.

Vocabulary from the Novel   This valuable feature is intended to be shared directly with students to aid them in their reading of the novel. Words in the novel that students are likely to be unfamiliar with are listed by chapter (or chapter grouping) in their order of appearance in the novel. Words are defined according to the context in which they are used in the novel. Two types of words appear in the *Vocabulary from the Novel* section: general vocabulary words with utilitarian value (i.e., words that should be a part of the students' working or recognition vocabularies) and specialized vocabulary words (idioms, foreign words and phrases, archaic or obsolete words, geographical terms, allusions, jargon terms, technical terms, and the like) that are peculiar to that novel and necessary for reading comprehension. General vocabulary words are preceded by an asterisk, alerting students to the fact that they may be held responsible for learning the meanings of these words. Most or all of the asterisked words will appear in the *Testing on the Novel* section of the Study Guide, in the Developing Vocabulary test.

You may wish to duplicate the entire vocabulary list and hand it out to your students prior to their reading of the novel, or give them the vocabulary lists in chapter-by-chapter order. Students' comprehension and retention of the words will increase if you discuss the vocabulary in class. A periodic review of the asterisked words from previous chapters may also be helpful.

Since no such list of vocabulary from a novel can be exhaustive or fulfill every classroom need, students should be urged to keep a school or college dictionary within easy reach as they read the novel, whether at home or in the classroom.

Plot Synopsis and Literary Focus   A complete plot synopsis (a summary of the novel's events) with an accompanying Literary Focus (a summary of what is happening on a literary level) is provided for each chapter (or chapter grouping) of the novel. This section, intended for teacher use only, is particularly helpful as a handy reference to the specific chapters in which various pivotal events occur, and as an assurance that the most important events and literary elements in each chapter are being covered. It is particularly time-saving and helpful if you are teaching the novel for the first time or have not read the novel in many years. The *Plot Synopsis and Literary Focus* may also provide you with suggestions for literary interpretation and serve as a source of ideas for focused instruction.

You will probably not wish to duplicate this section for your students because of the possibility that some students would substitute its use for a reading of the novel itself. However, at your discretion, the material may be shared with students for review, reteaching, or enrichment after the novel has been read and fully discussed in class.

Reading Guide Questions   This section provides three sets of questions that will aid students in arriving at their own understanding and interpretations of the novel. The first two sets of questions, Identifying Facts and Interpreting Meanings, appear after each chapter (or chapter grouping); the third set, The Novel as a Whole, appears at the very end of the section. Identifying Facts questions test literal understanding of the events in the chapter and serve to demonstrate whether the students read the work and understood its main events. Interpreting Meanings questions address higher-level critical thinking skills, asking students to interpret, make connections and inferences, predict, or draw conclusions about the material they have just read. The Novel as a Whole questions require students to make informed judgments about the novel they have just completed, drawing on the skills of analysis, synthesis, and evaluation.

The *Reading Guide Questions* are designed for maximum flexibility, and you can use them in several ways. The Identifying Facts and Interpreting Meanings questions accompanying the individual chapters may be duplicated for students prior to their reading of a chapter or section, enabling them to read the material with more focus and with more depth of understanding. Both sets of questions may be used orally for classroom discussion; alternatively, they can be written as homework or in-class assignments. Many Identifying Facts questions can be adapted to a true/false format to serve as quick objective "check tests"

or "pop quizzes" that test literal recall of events in the chapter(s) or section the students have read.

The Interpreting Meanings questions lend themselves to being recorded in a journal or Reading Log. Reading Logs—notebooks in which students record their creative, critical, and/or emotional responses to the text as they read—may be used interactively between student and teacher or student and peer (or peer response group), if you desire. Students should be encouraged to respond to at least some of the Interpreting Meanings questions in writing, even if such questions are used primarily as classroom discussion questions.

The Novel as a Whole questions at the end of the Reading Guide Questions section may also be used for class discussion, as in- or out-of-class writing assignments, or as part of an essay test. You may wish to save these broader questions as material for midterm or final exams.

Writing About the Novel   This section provides two categories of writing assignments: A Creative Response and A Critical Response. Assignments taken from both categories will enrich and broaden students' interpretations of the novel.

The assignments in A Creative Response ask students to take their understanding of the novel into new territory. For example, students may be asked to alter the ending of the novel or retell an important episode from a different point of view; they may be asked to write a synopsis of an imagined sequel to the novel or cast appropriate contemporary actors in the roles of the novel's main characters. Although imaginative and sometimes fanciful, these assignments enable students to creatively demonstrate a deep understanding of the elements of the novel they have just read.

The assignments in A Critical Response ask students to evaluate and analyze the novel by taking a more critical/analytical route. Students may, for example, be asked to respond to a critic's derogatory comments about the novel, supporting or refuting those comments with specific evidence from the book. They may be asked to compare and contrast two characters in the novel, or to demonstrate how the overall theme of a novel is captured in a recurring symbol.

You may opt to provide students with the entire *Writing About the Novel* list of activities and let them choose one assignment from each category to complete. Alternatively, you may select appropriate activities for individual students, according to their level of mastery. Additional activities may be assigned to students who work quickly, need an extra challenge, or desire extra credit. Some of the assignments in A Critical Response may be used to supplement discussion of the novel as a whole; other assignments may be suitable for a midterm or final exam.

Going Beyond the Novel   This section offers research projects and other major assignments that take the student beyond the novel itself. As in the preceding category, *Writing About the Novel*, these assignments fall under two categories: A Creative Response and A Critical Response.

Assignments under A Creative Response might ask students to write about such topics as an imaginary encounter between the protagonist of the novel they have just read and the protagonist from another, related novel, or write a letter of rebuttal to the head of a censorship group that finds the novel they have just completed to be unsuitable for high-school students. A typical assignment from A Critical Response might ask the students to research the life of the novel's author, find out more about the historical context that informs the novel's themes, or compare and contrast two novels by the same author.

As in the *Writing About the Novel* section, you may elect to have the students choose an assignment from one or both categories, assign an activity for extra credit, or use one or more of the activities as topics for the year's major research project.

Testing on the Novel   This section provides you with the following three kinds of tests, reproducible for classroom use:

- ○ Developing Vocabulary—An objective test on the general vocabulary words asterisked in the *Vocabulary from the Novel* section. Occasionally, a Study Guide will contain two or more complete Developing Vocabulary tests.
- ○ Understanding What Happened/Recognizing Elements of the Novel—An objective test based on literal recall of events in the novel and an understanding of the elements of the novel
- ○ Critical Thinking and Writing—Short essay questions covering interpretation, evaluation, and analysis of the novel

A suggested scoring system is provided for each test, and answers are given in the Answer Key in the back of the Study Guide.

Note: Although suggested point values are given for each question in the Critical Thinking and Writing test, some questions may warrant treatment at greater length than can easily be covered in a brief essay. Thus, you may wish to assign only one or two of the questions given, weighting them more heavily than the twenty or twenty-five points that is usual for questions on this test. For example, two questions may be assigned at fifty points each.

Answer Key   The Study Guide Answer Key is complete and extensive, providing answers not just to objective questions but also to subjective questions for which there is no one "correct" answer. This section provides answers or suggested responses to all *Reading Guide Questions* (Identifying Facts, Interpreting Meanings, and The Novel as a Whole), *Writing About the Novel* assignments, and *Testing on the Novel*'s Developing Vocabulary, Understanding What Happened/Recognizing Elements of the Novel, and Critical Thinking and Writing tests. Answers to the interpretive questions in these sections will of course vary, but suggestions are included for what the students' responses should include or achieve. Note that answers are usually not provided for *Going Beyond the Novel* creative and critical assignments, as these do not often lend themselves to suggested responses.

For Further Reading   This section is included for both teachers and students who wish to extend their reading or research. It lists, where applicable, additional works by the author, works about the author (biographical and autobiographical), critical texts and articles about the author and his or her work, and, occasionally, related works with a similar topic or theme that may be of interest to those who enjoyed the novel.

Approaches to Teaching the Novel

You may choose to approach the teaching of a novel for which an *Elements of the Novel* Study Guide is provided in one of three ways: through in-class individual reading, through an oral-reading in-class group approach, or through the traditional independent reading method detailed in the *Teaching the Novel* section of this Study Guide. The traditional method assumes that students will do a good deal of their reading of the novel outside of class, and that copies of the novel are available for them to take home. However, when there is only one classroom set of a novel available for use by several classes, you may have to stagger class times or employ the individual in-class or oral group method discussed in this section as an alternative teaching approaching.

The suggested teaching times discussed in this section are approximate and will, of course, vary with the size and abilities of a specific class. The suggestions offered are thus only basic guidelines for helping you to determine an appropriate reading schedule and teaching approach for your particular class.

In-Class Reading: The Individual Approach

If there is only one classroom set of a novel and the reading of the novel must take place entirely during class time, with each student reading by him or herself, you should plan for approximately one week (five days) to cover fifty to seventy-five pages of text in class. This estimated time depends upon the book's print size and number of lines per page, the complexity of the novel's content and the author's style, and your students' reading abilities. (A class composed of a majority of reluctant readers will require several additional days.) For example, a typical paperback edition of William Golding's *Lord of the Flies* runs approximately 184 pages, with as many as 40 lines per page. Golding's style (sentence structure and vocabulary) is sophisticated; there are subtle shifts in tone and point of view, a good deal of complex imagery that serves a symbolic function and informs the main theme, and many allusions that must be explained to students. These factors combine to require a heightened effort on the reader's part to achieve comprehension. On the other hand, the novel *A Separate Peace* by John Knowles, though it contains roughly the same number of pages, does not present the difficulties in reading comprehension that Golding's novel does, and thus will not take students as long to read. Knowles's style is less intellectually demanding than Golding's; his themes and symbolism are more overt and less complicated. The first-person narration of the novel provides a conversational tone that makes the material less intimidating and easier for students to identify with. The style and content both promote rapid reading and easier comprehension. Thus, whereas the first three chapters of *Lord of the Flies* could easily take in-class readers five class sessions to complete, the first *five* chapters of a novel such as *A Separate Peace* could be covered in the same length of time. At this approximate rate, then, an in-class individual reading of *Lord of the Flies* could take up to twenty class sessions; *A Separate Peace,* no more than fifteen or sixteen.

In-Class Reading: The Group Approach

Assuming your class's ability to work productively in small groups, you may decide to divide a class into groups of five or six students to read a novel orally, taking turns so that each member of the group gets a chance to read aloud. While this approach does create a certain noise level and takes longer (approximately five to seven days longer than the individual in-class reading approach), there are multiple benefits that you may wish to consider. Reluctant readers are less hesitant to read aloud in small groups, and students are not inclined to be unkindly critical of each other in such a setting. Indeed, the better readers often quietly help and encourage the reluctant readers, and students often turn out to be fine tutors to other students. In addition, this approach gives students much-needed practice in oral reading and teaches them valuable skills for cooperating with others to complete a given task. When students are given a daily schedule to follow, and when the success of a group is incumbent upon the contributions of all its members, students are more productive and more conscious of time factors—much more so than when they are simply told, "Read this novel by the end of next week." Daydreaming and passivity are discouraged, since students must be "on task" for the oral reading. And since all the group's members are responsible for the group's grade, there is more incentive for individual input and cooperation. Another benefit of the group approach is that it provides students with a support group that allows them to share and clarify their ideas about the responses to their reading.

The group approach also has benefits for you, the teacher, with regard to the volume of paperwork involved in teaching a novel in depth. Since the *Reading Guide Questions* in this Study Guide are answered by the group as a whole rather than written out by individual students, you will find a significant reduction in the volume of papers that you have to deal with—yet students still enjoy the benefit of exercising their critical thinking skills. Additionally, you need only make one set of photocopies of *Reading Guide Questions* per group as opposed to one per individual.

The following basic guidelines will help you to successfully implement the in-class group approach.

○ You should deliberately form groups based on a good match of better readers with more reluctant ones. Students should remain in the same groups throughout the reading of the novel.

○ Students should be provided with a reading schedule that tells them exactly how much material they are responsible for covering and by what date. Before they actually begin reading the novel, you should give them copies of any *Focusing on Background, Elements of the Novel,* and *Vocabulary from the Novel* material deemed necessary for an understanding of the novel they are about to read, as well as refer them to the *Handbook of Literary Terms* in their **Elements of Literature** Pupil's Edition for a review of important literary elements.

○ Each student should be assigned a numbered copy of the novel and provided with a numbered set of *Reading Guide Questions* as well. Students should use the same assigned materials each day and return them at the end of each class period. There should be approximately ten extra sets of these questions and ten extra copies of the novel for students who miss class to check out on an overnight basis. Students who miss class should work on their own until they are back "on track" again, according to the reading schedule.

○ Unless you have scheduled a quiz at the beginning of a class period, students should obtain their materials and immediately form their assigned groups upon entering the classroom. (**Note:** Chapter or section quizzes are not provided in the Study Guide; however, you can easily construct quizzes by adapting the *Reading Guide Questions'* Identifying Facts questions into an objective "check tests" format. You may dictate quizzes orally, limiting them to five true/false questions per chapter or chapter grouping. The answers should be checked immediately afterward by having students exchange papers.)

○ The *Reading Guide Questions* should be answered in writing, and students should use complete sentences. A different member of the group should act as recorder of responses for each chapter or chapter grouping. The group should review their answers and make any necessary changes/revisions before the responses are submitted to you for evaluation. There should be a labeled folder for each group; group members should place the *Reading Guide Question* responses—whether they are in-progress or completed—in their assigned folder at the end of each class period. At times, it may be appropriate for students to answer the Interpreting Meanings questions in a journal or Reading Log as homework assignments.

○ Groups that are able to move at a faster pace than the schedule calls for should be allowed to do so. You may determine what reward these groups receive— perhaps in-class time for leisure reading.

○ After groups have completed their reading of the novel, they should discuss the questions under The Novel as a Whole. It may be interesting to see what insights the various groups have come up with by having the class as a whole discuss their responses to these questions.

Following is a model Reading Schedule of the type you may wish to create and provide for students involved in an in-class reading group. This model is based on a novel of medium length—the twelve-chapter-long *Lord of the Flies*—and may be adapted to novels of varying lengths.

Day 1: Read orally the *Reading Guide Questions* (hereinafter labeled *RGQ*) for Chapter One. Begin the oral reading of Chapter One.

Day 2: Complete the reading of Chapter One. Begin answering the *RGQ* for Chapter One.

Day 3: Complete the answers to the *RGQ* for Chapter One, review them, make needed changes and corrections, and turn them in.

Day 4: Quiz on Chapter One—optional. Read the *RGQ* for Chapter Two. Begin reading Chapter Two.

Day 5: Complete reading of Chapter Two. Answer the *RGQ* and turn them in.

Day 6: Quiz on Chapter Two—optional. Read the *RGQ* for Chapter Three. Read Chapter Three. Answer the *RGQ* and turn them in.

Day 7: Quiz on Chapter Three—optional. Read the *RGQ* for Chapter Four. Begin reading Chapter Four.

Day 8: Complete reading of Chapter Four. Answer the *RGQ* and turn them in.

Day 9: Quiz on Chapter Four—optional. Read the *RGQ* for Chapter Five. Begin reading Chapter Five.

Day 10: Complete reading of Chapter Five. Answer the *RGQ* and turn them in.

Day 11: Quiz on Chapter Five—optional. Read the *RGQ* for Chapter Six. Begin reading Chapter Six.

Day 12: Complete reading of Chapter Six. Answer the *RGQ* and turn them in.

Day 13: Quiz on Chapter Six—optional. Read the *RGQ* for Chapter Seven. Begin reading Chapter Seven.

Day 14: Complete reading of Chapter Seven. Answer the *RGQ* and turn them in.

Day 15: Quiz on Chapter Seven—optional. Read the *RGQ* for Chapter Eight. Begin reading Chapter Eight.

Day 16: Complete reading of Chapter Eight. Begin answering the *RGQ*.

Day 17: Complete answering the *RGQ* for Chapter Eight and turn them in. Quiz on Chapter Eight— optional.

Day 18: Read the *RGQ* for Chapter Nine. Read Chapter Nine.

Day 19: Answer the *RGQ* for Chapter Nine and turn them in.

Day 20: Quiz on Chapter Nine—optional. Read the *RGQ* for Chapter Ten. Begin reading Chapter Ten.

Day 21: Complete reading of Chapter Ten. Answer the *RGQ* and turn them in.

Day 22: Quiz on Chapter Ten—optional. Read the *RGQ* for Chapter Eleven. Begin reading Chapter Eleven.

Day 23: Complete reading of Chapter Eleven. Answer the *RGQ* and turn them in.

Day 24: Quiz on Chapter Eleven—optional. Read the *RGQ* for Chapter Twelve. Begin reading Chapter Twelve.

Day 25: Complete reading of Chapter Twelve. Begin answering the *RGQ*.

Day 26: Complete answering the *RGQ* for Chapter Twelve and turn them in.

Day 27: Quiz on Chapter Twelve—optional. Begin discussion of The Novel as a Whole questions.

Independent Reading

If each student has a copy of the novel being studied, then outside reading—including the use of the *Reading Guide Questions* and written answers to them—should take at least a week less than the total number of days the Individual In-Class Reading method would require, assuming that about an hour of homework per night is expected.

Since Study Guides are available for several different novels at each grade level, students may be allowed to read an "extra" novel as a completely independent assign-ment. You may wish to select the novel that is most appro-priate to the abilities and interests of the student; this is especially important for reluctant readers, so that they will be assured of success. Both the *Vocabulary from the Novel* and the *Reading Guide Questions* should be given to the student before he or she begins the independent reading. Instead of testing the student, you may wish to have him or her complete one or more of the activities provided in the *Writing About the Novel* or *Going Beyond the Novel* sections of the Study Guide to culminate the student's independent effort.

Focusing on Background

The Life and Work of John Knowles (1926–   )

Born on September 16, 1926, in Fairmont, West Virginia, John Knowles was educated at Phillips Exeter Academy and at Yale, from which he graduated in 1949 with a B.A. in English. Knowles, the son of James Myron Knowles and the former Mary Beatrice Shea, dedicated his first novel, *A Separate Peace,* "To Bea and Jim with gratitude and love."

After graduation from Yale, Knowles worked for two years in Connecticut as a reporter for the Hartford *Courant.* From 1952–56, he was a freelance writer, living and traveling in Europe, primarily in France, Italy, and Greece. Following that, Knowles worked as an associate editor for *Holiday* magazine. All of these experiences were, according to Knowles, preparation for doing what he considered his life's work: writing. Then, in 1960, in the United States, Knowles published *A Separate Peace,* which won the Rosenthal Award of the National Institute of Arts and Letters and the William Faulkner Foundation Award. After this success, Knowles became a full-time writer.

When Knowles finished writing *A Separate Peace* and finally found a British publisher after having been turned down by every significant American publisher, he calculated that the book would sell, at best, about 3,000 copies. Twenty-five years and nine million copies later, Knowles refutes the notion that such overwhelming success with a first book is a curse: "It freed me from having to teach school or be a journalist, enabling me to devote myself entirely to fiction writing. And it gave me a public identity."

Knowles has been writer-in-residence at both Princeton University and at the University of North Carolina. He is frequently a lecturer for university audiences across the nation. In addition to a travelogue and a collection of short stories, Knowles has published several other novels. He currently lives in eastern Long Island, where he continues to write.

The Critical Response to the Novel

When *A Separate Peace* was published in Britain by Secket and Warburg of London, it received critical acclaim there. Soon thereafter, the book was published in the United States by the Macmillan Company. It sold about 7,000 copies, over twice the number Knowles had anticipated, and received glowing praise from the American critics as well. Six years later, in 1966, the book was printed as a paperback by Bantam Books, Inc. As it became a favorite among young readers all across the United States, establishing itself along with Salinger's *The Catcher in the Rye* and Golding's *Lord of the Flies,* sales increased dramatically, and, as Knowles comments, the book "became public property." Knowles's reaction to the book's success is that, "It was what the book deserved . . . because it did tend to acquire a destiny apart from mine, and I feel about it the way a parent with a rather workaday existence must feel when he finds he has produced a world-beating child: a slight sense of wonder, pride, and a certain detachment." He adds that the book, which has sold between 250,000 and 400,000 thousand copies every year, is his "annuity, the

faithful offspring who will keep me in my old age."

Much commentary has been devoted to comparing both Knowles and his novel to J. D. Salinger and his *The Catcher in the Rye.* One critic responded that Knowles had written his novel as though "he had never heard of J. D. Salinger." Another remarked that, "Some reviewers have proposed that *A Separate Peace* compares with J. D. Salinger's *The Catcher in the Rye.* It doesn't." On this matter, Knowles himself explains that, although Salinger's book had been published a few years previously, he had never read it. When he was about one-third of the way into his own book, he got a copy of Salinger's and read about ten pages. Realizing that he might let Salinger's work influence his, since both are about a teenage boy in a prep school, he put it aside and didn't finish it until his own was in galleys. Knowles comments, "Then I read it and admired it very much. They are very different books. His is a 360-degree circumambulating of one fascinating character. Mine is linear, a narrative involving two and then four interrelating characters.''

Of the enduring nature of his novel, Knowles states, ''The book has affected millions of lives, influenced them deeply, modified what they saw and felt in the world about them. The ultimate importance of *A Separate Peace* is that it has reached out to the readers who need it.'' Although *A Separate Peace* received high praise upon its release in both Britain and the United States, some reviewers tempered their praise of it with reservations about various aspects of the novel. Following is a sampling of critical reception of the novel.

> Without sentimentality and with moving perceptiveness, the novel deftly recreates a personal relationship and a campus increasingly touched by the restiveness of war.
>
> —from *Booklist*
> February 15, 1960

> It is a well-conceived, well-written novel, with levels of meaning not possible to explore briefly. There are moments when I do not fully believe Mr. Knowles' structure, but these passing skepticisms do not weaken the major truths in this excellent book.
>
> —from *New York Times Book Review,* February 7, 1960
> Edmund Fuller

> I make no reservations whatever about this book. It is a beautifully written story. For style and imagery, *A Separate Peace* ranks with the work of the very best young American novelists, such as William Styron. At the same time it has none of the false symbolism which so many Americans employ in an attempt to add depth to their work . . . Mr. Knowles' book has great depth. Here we may read messages which only become clear much later, after we have pondered long over the disturbing allegories. The interpretation of the messages must be highly subjective, which holds true of all major works of art.
>
> —from *San Francisco Chronicle,* June 26, 1960
> Douglas Aitke

> A short, thoughtful, ambitious American study of a fatal relationship . . . Mr. Knowles has clearly worked hard on this novel, modeling it carefully on the best neo-Forsterian, Trillingesque lines. Yet somehow it just fails to convince . . . Gene and Finny seem to be performing their odd psychological warfare in a vacuum. Gene is particularly unsatisfactory; he has almost

> none of the ego-sense that you expect in a first-person narrator and it makes him difficult to identify with.
>
> —from *New Statesman,* May 2, 1959
> Maurice Richardson

> A novel of altogether exceptional power and distinction . . . Mr. Knowles's world is the real world where black-and-white character-contrasts rarely lie conveniently to hand. Gene and Finny can slip in and out of each other's roles and yet remain entirely themselves while doing so. Their relationship has that subtle elusiveness which is entirely human and which novelists, with good reason, find desperately difficult to convey . . . There is no gush. There is no smut. If this is Mr. Knowles's first novel it shows an astonishingly firm grasp of the right end of the stick.
>
> —*London Times Literary Supplement,* May 1, 1959

> One more foray into the territory of guilt earned in adolescence. This novel is painstakingly ambitious enough to fall short of success, but it suggests what it means to achieve.
>
> —from *Commonweal,* December 9, 1960
> Jean Holzhauer

> Original and arresting story . . . Although Finny is never completely credible and although the mock trial at the end seems contrived, this book rates high indeed because of the directness of the writing, the authenticity of the school setting, the absolute reality of the tensions, fears, almost unbearable exuberance these adolescents experience as they develop. For the older group mature enough to appreciate the author's skill as well as the emotions and actions of the characters.
>
> —from *Horn Book,* October 1960
> M. C. Scoggin

> Here is (if you want to look at it that way) a simple tale about school boys, and on that level the book is entertaining enough. But the character of Finny stays in the mind and the more one thinks about him, the more meaning he has.
>
> —from *Saturday Review,* March 5, 1960
> Granville Hicks

Study Guide: A Separate Peace

The Source of the Story

In an article written in 1985 to celebrate the twenty-fifth anniversary of *A Separate Peace,* Knowles states that the novel is indeed autobiographical, not in its portrayal of incidents but in the sense that "the emotional truth of it comes out of my [Knowles's] life." He explains that he "wrote the book to dramatize and work through" a number of questions he had had when he was a student at Phillips Exeter Academy during the summer session of 1943. In addition to whether he and his classmates would participate in the war, other questions were, ". . . what was war, and what was aggression, and what were loyalty and rivalry, what were goodness and hate and fear and idealism," questions intensified by World War II.

Knowles acknowledges that he modeled Gene Forrester, the narrator of the novel, after himself and that Phineas was modeled after an exceptionally athletic classmate named David Hackett, who was a student at Exeter only that one summer session. However, David Hackett, who went on to work in the Justice Department for Robert Kennedy, was not crippled by a fall from a tree. Knowles explains that he himself had been injured in an accident, which hadn't been very serious, and that he turned his real accident into Finny's "fateful fictional one." Wanting to show the "darker streaks of human nature," Knowles states that he had to make Phineas the victim. Other characters in the novel were loosely based on other classmates at Exeter. Brinker Hadley, for example, was patterned after Gore Vidal.

Elements of the Novel

The Themes of *A Separate Peace*

As the author himself states, the novel deals with a number of significant issues such as war, aggression, loyalty, rivalry, goodness, hate, fear, and idealism. On one level the book is an account of Gene Forrester's private war with himself. On other levels, the novel is an exploration of the forces that cause individuals to "sight the enemy" and construct, at "infinite cost" to themselves, lines of defense against "this enemy they thought they saw across the frontier." Knowles states, "It is a schoolboy story and it is also an allegory about the sources of war," adding, "It is a story of growth through tragedy."

Only through Gene's confrontation with his desire to destroy, his acknowledgment of his "darker streak of human nature," is he able to achieve an understanding of himself and find his own "separate peace." Near the end of Chapter 7, Gene states, "There was always something deadly lurking in anything I wanted, anything I loved. And if it wasn't there, as for example with Phineas, then I put it there myself." Gene grows through having to deal with tragedy, through his admission that he alone was responsible for having broken Finny's "harmonious and natural unity," that he had acted on his imagined, unfounded rivalry with his "best pal." He faces his dark side and knows that his betrayal of Finny was a result of "some ignorance inside me, some crazy thing inside me, something blind." Before Gene enters the war, he has an insight that even many "mature" adults never have. He knows from his own personal experience, from his own personal struggle, that wars result from the same source as his betrayal of Finny: "they were not made by generations and their special stupidities, but . . . were made instead by something ignorant in the human heart."

Gene states that his war ended before he ever put on a uniform because he had already killed his enemy at school. Having acknowledged to himself, just before he caused Finny to fall from the tree, that Finny was never and could never be his rival, his "enemy," the one Gene had killed at school was not Finny: it was his own ignorance and innocence. With that realization, Gene was able to bury his anger, his fury, and enter the war without hatred. Through his personal tragedy, through his confrontation with, and defeat of, his own "ignorance," Gene triumphs, finally achieving the harmony that he had destroyed in Finny. He is, at last, able to live, without "an obsessive labor of defense," as Finny had so naturally done.

Gene Forrester is a teenager at a prestigious prep school. Nonetheless, Gene's personal "rite of passage" clearly illustrates the author's message: there can be no end to aggression and war and rivalry and hate, there can be no freedom on a worldwide scale, until each individual can confront and conquer the "ignorance" in his or her own heart—that fear of imagined enemies.

The Setting

The physical and historical settings of *A Separate Peace* are an integral part of the story. Both come directly from Knowles's experiences as a student, and both indeed fostered the questions that he sought to explore in this work. A boys' prep school is an extremely contained structure. It has many formal and traditional rules of behavior regarding academics, sports competition, and general school conduct, plus the tacit and almost more important code of conduct among peers. The double pressure is tremendous, especially to an adolescent. The additional weight of wartime adds an even greater urgency to an already explosive situation.

Although Knowles creates "Devon School," the setting of the novel is clearly his own alma mater, Phillips Exeter Academy in New Hampshire. In his review of the novel for the *New Yorker*, critic Whitney Ballett stated, ". . . Indeed, to anyone who has a nodding acquaintance with the institution, it is Exeter, down to the last ivy leaf and lights-out-time," a fact about which, "the Academy, though it would never be indecorous enough to admit it, should be pleased." Appropriately, when the novel was produced as a movie by Paramount in 1972, it was filmed at Exeter Academy.

Point of View

Knowles employs the first-person point of view to tell his story. Gene Forrester is the narrator, and the reader learns only what Gene chooses to tell. He uses the pronoun *I*, and his observations and thoughts may not always inspire believability because they are so one-sided. He does eventually admit to sometimes coming to the wrong conclusions.

The events of the novel are described by a Gene who is more mature than the schoolboy of the story, because he has had fifteen years in which to reflect on his experiences.

Style

The tone of *A Separate Peace* is set through its literary style. The language is educated, perhaps even a bit elite; certainly appropriate for the student at an Eastern prep school. Knowles uses moody description, imagery, and figures of speech liberally throughout the story, yet somehow maintains a slight aloofness. Perhaps this, too, is appropriate, as most of the novel is told as a flashback, and the narrator would no longer have a total sense of immediacy about the events. Gene's many descriptions of the school buildings, the seasons, the other boys, and Finny have an almost dreamlike quality.

The Characters

Where some novels create mainly an emotional impact, *A Separate Peace* creates an intellectual one. Despite the occurrence of highly charged emotions and incidents—joy, jealousy, madness, and death—the narrator never truly expresses a depth of emotions. He never cries over Finny; he never so much as shakes his hand in friendship. He treasures and mulls over emotions in his mind, letting only certain bits sift out as he becomes capable of handling them. The story is allegorical, and the characters go through their motions as symbols, almost mechanically, especially the two main characters, Gene and Finny. The over-sensitive Leper and the disillusioned Brinker perhaps seem the most truly human.

In this psychological study of Gene Forrester's internal battle with his own "ignorance" of heart, and by extension that of mankind's as well, the most important literary element in *A Separate Peace* becomes the development of the protagonist's and antagonist's characters. It is through Gene's individual struggle to come to terms with his own "dark" nature, in his private war against Phineas, his ideal, that Knowles drives home the message of the novel: If Gene is, as his classmate Leper accuses him of being, "savage underneath," so, then, are we all.

Gene Forrester, the narrator and protagonist of the novel, recalls his experiences at Devon, an exclusive boys' prep school in New Hampshire, when he was a student there during 1942 and 1943. He is a short, intellectual sixteen-year-old who is wary of being "taken in" by anyone or anything. Gene determines that Finny, who excels at athletics, and he will be "even" if he can graduate at the top of their class.

Phineas (Finny), the antagonist of the novel, is Gene's unique and free-spirited classmate and roommate at Devon. Finny is also short, but muscular and graceful. He is handsome, with striking green eyes, and is the essence of the careless peace. Finny considers Gene his "best pal."

Brinker Hadley, one of the Devon students, is a class leader. He is a tall boy with a face that is all straight lines. He is politically inclined, somewhat conservative, and very concerned about doing the proper thing in any situation. He attempts to explore the facts about Finny's accident.

Leper (Elwin Lepellier) is a "naturalist." He is small, with very fair skin and a thin face, and he wears steel-rimmed glasses. He is quiet, intent in his own world of birds and beaver dams, until he becomes the first Devon student to enlist in the army, and Devon's first "war casualty." He "escapes" from the army rather than take a Section Eight (insanity) discharge.

Chet Douglas, Bobby Zane, and Brownie Perkins are other students whose roles in the novel are minor. They each exemplify the perfect Devon student: obliging and considerate, therefore having no hope of being "somebody."

Cliff Quackenbush is the rowing crew manager, a "macho" character. He is disliked by most of the boys, since he is arrogant and prone to fighting. He and Gene clash during the winter term.

Mr. Prud'homme, Mr. Patch-Withers, and Mr. Ludsbury are Devon teachers. Mr.

Prud'homme is a substitute Master for the summer; he is easily won over by Finny's charm. Mr. Patch-Withers is the sternest of the Masters, filling in for the Headmaster during the summer. His face changes colors continually, much to the interest and amusement of the boys. Mr. Ludsbury is a regular staff member, with a British accent and an exaggerated Adam's-apple.

Dr. Stanpole is the kind-hearted school physician who treats Finny's injured leg and who advises Gene on how to best help Finny.

Phil Latham is the school wrestling coach. He appears infrequently in the story.

Mr. Hadley, Brinker's father, is a proponent of the notion that one's greatest privilege and greatest moment is to serve one's country, and that one's goal should be to achieve a "military record you can be proud of."

Symbolism

One pervasive symbol in the novel is the tree. Although Knowles doesn't specifically reveal what it symbolizes, its importance to and throughout the novel indicates his intent that it serve as one. One possible interpretation is that it symbolizes, as did the tree in the Garden of Eden, man's fall from perfection. Gene perceives Finny as a perfect being, one who is of superior quality to himself and all others. After Finny's fall from the tree, he is, of course, crippled; this makes him more "human" in Gene's eyes. Ironically, after his jump immediately following Finny's fall, Gene is free of fear for the first time. Subsequently, Gene, through his internal struggle with himself, achieves a heightened state of "perfection," as he confronts and conquers the ignorance in his own human heart.

Some readers have suggested that Finny is a symbolic Christ figure whose betrayal and "crucifixion" by his best pal ultimately lead to Gene's redemption. He himself becomes like Finny—one who doesn't hate or fear. Since Knowles has classified his story as allegorical, it follows then that his characters serve symbolic functions. Finny, symbolizes the good in mankind, the accepting, non-fearful, non-judgmental, non-competitive (except in the circumscribed world of sports) human being. His foil, Gene, embodies what Knowles terms "the darker streaks of human nature": jealousy, rivalry, aggression, hate, and fear. The world's "gentle souls" who, when faced with the grotesque elements of reality, can cope only by escaping into some form of mental illness, are represented by Leper. He wonders, and rightfully so perhaps, if it is he who is "psycho" or if, in truth, it is the army that is. Brinker, who progresses from the class leader who first declares he will enlist in the service to one who resents having to fight a war his father's "crowd" is responsible for, represents those individuals who, because of some change in perspective, become disillusioned with their former ideals. Because Brinker takes it upon himself to investigate Finny's accident, he also symbolizes, as Gene labels him, "Justice incarnate."

Foreshadowing

Finny's tragedy is skillfully foreshadowed throughout the novel. In the second chapter, at the tea, Gene secretly hopes that Finny won't always get away with everything. Later, in the same chapter, Finny invents the Suicide Club, and then, to complete the circle of tension, Gene nearly falls from the tree. He is saved by Finny in a scene that is also ironic, because it is Gene who will later cause Finny to fall.

In Chapter Eight, after Finny returns with cast and crutches, the description of the waves again foreshadows further complications. The trial at the end of the novel is also hinted at halfway through the story, when Brinker stages the first "inquiry" in the Butt room. The reader knows, along with Gene, that Brinker is unlikely to let the matter drop.

Teaching the Novel

Introducing the Novel/ Pacing the Assignment

You may wish to give the students a review of literary terms that will be used in discussing the novel (see *Elements of the Novel*), including a brief review of the terms *allegory* and *symbolism*. Students should be introduced to the novel's setting: Devon School, a boys' prep school in New Hampshire, during World War II in 1942–1943). They should be told that the novel is an allegory and that as such, the characters may be viewed as symbolic figures. No unusual dialects figure in the novel, just a few French terms appear, but it may be helpful to cover the connotations of some of the more difficult vocabulary words which may be found in the section, *Vocabulary from the Novel*. The students should also be made aware of the author's use of description and imagery so that they can watch for it as they read.

An introductory discussion might focus on the ideas of friendship and peer-pressure during a person's high-school years. Students probably have strong opinions about their criteria for friendship, and about the kinds of people that they don't associate with, along with causes of jealousy in friendships and ways of expressing loyalty. Such a discussion would lead naturally into the themes and characters of the novel.

A Separate Peace is a work of medium length consisting of thirteen chapters. The action is not hard to follow, but the characterizations need to be covered with special attention. Students should be encouraged to take notes on the characters, and especially to notice all the ways in which Gene and Finny are presented as opposites. They may even wish to make a comparison and contrast chart in order to carry out a "trait analysis" of the two characters.

The first two chapters of the novel are short and may be taught together. In them, the story is established as a flashback (you may wish to explain and discuss the concept of a framing device), and the relaxed summer session is set as the scene for the unfolding of Gene's and Finny's relationship.

Each of the following nine chapters (up to Chapter 12) probably requires separate teaching sessions. The students' understanding of the personalities and motivations of the main characters will be augmented by detailed discussions of the many clues presented in these chapters. The supporting characters, Leper and Brinker, also need to be considered carefully. Is quiet Leper more closely akin to Gene or Finny? Could Brinker, too, be considered a foil to one of the main characters?

The last two chapters, though brief, present the climax and the resolution of the story. The teacher is the best judge in deciding how much time the students will need to assimilate the concepts in the conclusion.

Motivating and Aiding Student Reading

Some students may readily identify with the characters, circumstances, and events in *A Separate Peace*, while others may find it far removed from their own experience and interests. Any or all of the following questions might motivate students to think about and react to the novel they are about to read.

1. One of the themes presented in the novel is that of envy between friends. What are some possible causes of jealousy between friends? Is envy necessarily a negative emotion, or could it sometimes produce positive results?

2. The students at Devon are forced to deal with the subject of war, and therefore also to consider the opposite of war, peace. What is your definition of peace? How would you characterize world peace? What would your own personal "separate" peace consist of? Are any of the elements of your two answers similar?

3. If you began to suspect your best friend of trying to thwart your plans for reaching some goal, how would you deal with the problem? What if you still cared about your friend, even though you felt betrayed?

4. The United States has not been directly threatened by attack in this generation's lifetime, although the presence of poised nuclear weapons is keenly felt. Considering this, and the war in Vietnam, do you agree or disagree with the following theory that will be raised

in this novel: that war isn't real, that it's just an insider's joke, created by those in power to keep young people in their places.

5. This novel takes place in a boys' prep school: there are no female characters. What are your expectations of what life in a private boys' school would be like? Would the tensions and relationships there be any different from those in a coed public school?

Vocabulary from the Novel

Words are listed by chapter in their order of appearance. Words preceded by an asterisk (*) are general vocabulary words that may appear in *Testing on the Novel:* Developing Vocabulary.

Chapter 1

*tacit — unvoiced or unspoken; understood without being openly expressed

*contentious — controversial; argumentative; quarrelsome

lacrosse — a game played by two teams with a ball and long-handled netted racquets

*irate — enraged

*inveigle — to entice or lure by artful talk

*consternation — a sudden, alarming amazement or dread

*rhetorically — spoken in a manner not intended to elicit a reply

seigneurs — feudal lords

*collaborator — one who works or cooperates with an enemy

Chapter 2

*eloquence — fluent, forceful speech

*indulgent — yielding to the wishes or desires of (oneself or another)

*essence — the basic or intrinsic quality of a thing

*inane — lacking sense or ideas; empty or void

*resonant — deep and full of sound

*pun — a play on words where both have the same sound, but different meanings

*conniver — one who gives aid to wrongdoing by pretending not to know or notice

*infer — to conclude by reasoning from premises or evidence

Chapter 3

*venerable — respected due to great age or associated dignity

*inured — toughened or accustomed to by extended experience

*anarchy — a state of society without government or law

fey — strange or otherworldly

*insidious — treacherous; marked by hidden dangers, hazards or perils

blitzkrieg (German) — an overwhelming all-out attack

Chapter 4

*enmity — active and typically mutual hatred or ill will

*vulnerable — open to attack or damage

*treachery — violation of allegiance or faith or confidence; the betrayal of a trust

*candid — free from bias, prejudice, or malice; frank; absence of deception

*jounced — moved in an up-and-down manner; bounced

Chapter 5

cordovan — a soft fine-grained colored leather

*delirious — marked by delirium, a mental disturbance characterized by confusion, disordered speech, and hallucinations

decalogue — a basic set of rules carrying binding authority

*ludicrous — amusing or laughable through obvious absurdity, incongruity, exaggeration or eccentricity

*irresolutely — uncertainly; without sureness

*erratic — inconsistent; irregular

Chapter 6

*vindicated — freed; delivered from

*idiosyncratic — peculiarly individualistic; eccentric

*invoking — petitioning for help or support; appealing to

sinecure — an office or position requiring little or no work and usually providing an income

bantam — diminutive or tiny

automaton — a robot; one who acts in a monotonous, routine manner

*__catapulted__ — thrown or launched as if by a catapult (an ancient device for hurling missiles)

*__reprimand__ — a severe or formal rebuke or disapproval

*__stupefaction__ — overwhelmed amazement

Chapter 7

*__impinge__ — to come into close contact with; encroach; infringe

*__insinuating__ — tending to cause doubt, distrust, or change of outlook

*__fratricide__ — the act of murdering one's own brother or sister

*__judiciously__ — wisely; in a soundly judgmental manner

*__funereal__ — of or relating to a funeral

contretemps — an inopportune embarrassing occurrence; mishap

*__conspiratorial__ — of or relating to or suggestive of a conspiracy or plot

knickers — loose-fitting short pants gathered at the knee

puttees — cloth strips wrapped around the leg from ankle to knee; leather leggings secured by a strap or laces

*__elite__ — the choice part; a socially superior group

*__futility__ — sense of purposelessness; fruitlessness

*__virtuoso__ — one who excels in the technique of an art; especially a highly skilled musical performer (as on the violin)

khaki — a cloth, of a dull yellowish brown color, made of cotton or wool and used especially for military uniforms

*__encumbrance__ — something that burdens or weighs down; an impediment

Chapter 8

clodhoppers — large, heavy shoes

*__ambiguously__ — doubtfully; uncertainly; obscurely

*__sanctity__ — a holiness of life and character; godliness

*__discernible__ — detectible with the eyes or with the other senses; discriminating

*__opulent__ — amply or plentifully provided; luxurious; rich

*__sobriety__ — the quality or state of being abstinent, sober, or well-balanced

*__aphorisms__ — concise statements of principle; adages; maxims

*__pungent__ — sharp or biting to the sense of taste or smell

*__preeminently__ — outstandingly; supremely

*__poignance__ — that which painfully affects the feelings; that which touches or pierces

*__refuting__ — overthrowing by argument, evidence, or proof; disproving

gulls — people who are easily deceived or cheated; dupes

*__patriarchal__ — old; fatherly

*__profound__ — penetrating to the depth of one's being; pervasive; thorough

*__cranium__ — the part of the skull that encloses the brain

gibe — taunting words; scoffs

*__abashed__ — embarrassed; disconcerted

*__sententiousness__ — state of excessive moralizing

*__gullible__ — easily deceived, cheated, or duped

Chapter 9

*__vagaries__ — eccentric or unpredictable manifestations, actions, or notions

herringbone — to ascend a slope by toeing out on skis and placing the weight on the inner edge

Bolsheviks — members of the extremist wing of the Russian Social Democratic party in Russia that seized supreme power in the 1917–1920 Revolution

*__liaison__ — a close bond or connection; an interrelationship

*__multifariously__ — varyingly; diversely

dowager — a widow holding property or title received from her dead husband

*__cacophony__ — harsh or discordant sound; dissonance

proviso — an article or clause that introduces a condition; a stipulation

Study Guide: A Separate Peace

accolade — a mark of acknowledgment; an award

Chorus (in a Greek tragedy) — a group of actors performing in unison as one character whose functions include, among others, embodying the moral ideas of society and admonishing characters against breaking these moral laws

Chapter 10

* **holocaust** — a thorough destruction or devastation, especially by fire

* **austerity** — the quality or state of being stern and forbidding in appearance and manner; the quality of being somber or grave

aesthete — one having or affecting sensitivity to the beautiful, especially in art

* **foreboding** — an omen, prediction, or presentiment especially of coming evil; a portent

furlough — a leave of absence from duty granted especially to a soldier

* **imperceptibly** — slightly; gradually; subtly

Chapter 11

* **preposterous** — contrary to nature, reason, or common sense; absurd

eunuch — a castrated man placed in charge of a harem

* **latent** — dormant; quiescent

* **bane** — a person or thing that harms, spoils, or ruins

* **incredulously** — skeptically; unbelievingly

* **ruefully** — mournfully; regretfully

* **flourish** — to grow luxuriantly; to thrive

* **torpidly** — dormantly; numbly; apathetically

* **urbane** — notably polite or finished in manner; polished

* **incarnate** — to give bodily form and substance to; to realize; to actualize

* **obstinate** — not easily subdued, remedied, or removed

Chapter 12

pontiff — bishop; pope

* **incongruity** — the state of being incompatible; lack of harmony

* **irreconcilably** — inconsistently; inharmoniously; uncompromisingly

* **impervious** — incapable of being influenced or affected

* **parody** — a feeble or ridiculous imitation

* **languid** — drooping from exhaustion; weak

* **precariously** — doubtfully; dangerously; insecurely

Chapter 13

* **bellicose** — inclined to start quarrels or warfare; belligerent

* **disconcerting** — disturbing; unsettling

* **parry** — to ward off a weapon or blow

Plot Synopsis and Literary Focus

Chapter 1: The narrator, Gene Forrester, returns to Devon School after fifteen years, especially desirous to see the marble stairs in the First Academy Building and one particular tree along the Devon River bank, both of which he states are "fearful sites." After seeing both, Gene observes that nothing endures and declares that he, too, is now changed. At this point, the story flashes back to the summer of 1942 when Gene, his roommate Phineas (Finny), and others were attending a Summer Session at Devon, established to accelerate graduation and produce a supply of soldiers for World War II. During this Session, Finny establishes an unprecedented custom for the Upper Middlers—jumping from the limb of a huge tree into the river below. Only Finny finds the experience exhilarating. None of the other boys jumps from the tree, except Gene, who defers to Finny's influence. The resulting closeness between Gene and Finny causes Gene to feel they are the best of friends.

Literary Focus: Since the story is told from the perspective of an adult, fifteen years after he was a teenager at Devon School, the "rite of passage" motif is clearly established. In addition, the author emphasizes the frame he will use for the novel: beginning his story in the present, the narrator flashes back to the past, to the summer of 1942. The reader should anticipate that the narrator will complete the frame, after sharing his experiences and his conclusions, by ending his story where he begins it, in the present.

Chapter 2: Because of the war, and partly because of Finny's inability to adhere to school regulations, the faculty relaxes its hold on the students, whom Gene describes as "careless and wild." Finny's particular brand of individuality is illustrated in his choice of dress for the traditional term tea: his pink shirt is his "emblem" to celebrate the recent bombing of Central Europe; his belt is the Devon School tie, which he explains connects Devon to the world and to the war and shows the school's involvement in everything. Gene, who observes that Finny can get away with anything, admits to himself that he feels a little envious, adding that there is no harm in envying one's best friend a little. After the tea, Finny suggests that he and Gene go jump from the tree. Gene, as usual, succumbs. The two of them name their "club" the Super Suicide Society of the Summer Session. While on the branch, Gene loses his bal-

ance, but Finny saves him from falling by grabbing his arm. Later, Gene reflects that he might have been killed and that Finny had practically saved his life.

Literary Focus: Knowles establishes the characters of his symbolic, allegorical protagonist (the narrator, Gene) and antagonist (Finny) in this chapter. In view of the author's conception of the novel as allegory, the reader should consider the two characters not only as individuals in a story about schoolboys but as contrasting aspects of human nature. An additional contrast the reader should note is the author's juxtaposition of the peace of this summer session with the war (World War II) raging in the outside world.

Chapter 3: Although Finny is presented as the symbol of the "good," or the "balanced man," the goal of human evolution, he also has his unpleasant side. He has a way of forcing others to follow his lead, to grow against their will, before they're ready. He seems to contain the seeds of his own destruction.

Upon further reflection, Gene realizes that Finny is to blame for endangering his life. However, Gene continues to participate in the nightly meetings of the club in order to please Finny. Finny continues to express his individuality by inventing a new game, blitzball, which meets with great success. One day Finny breaks a school swimming record, which only he and Gene witness. After Finny makes Gene promise to say nothing about it, Gene begins to perceive Finny in a new light, as one too unusual for rivalry, the basis of most relationships at Devon. When Finny then suggests that he and Gene go to the beach, Gene agrees in spite of the risk of being expelled from school and the certainty that he will fail an important test the next day. Before they fall asleep on the beach that night, Finny declares that Gene is his best pal. Gene, however, is unable to reciprocate the feeling, held back by some deeper level of feeling containing the truth.

Literary Focus: Gene begins the journey into himself with his consideration of the extent of Finny's influence over him. However, it is only a beginning since Gene fights with himself between remaining loyal to Finny and feeling resentment of Finny's power over him. After Finny breaks the swimming record, Gene's resentment of Finny is heightened when he begins to perceive Finny as something

Study Guide: A Separate Peace

superhuman, a "god" whom one must either fear or worship or deny and betray. Gene's confusion about his approach to this dilemma is evidenced by his inability to reciprocate Finny's courageous display of friendship at the beach.

This chapter contains a passage in which the mature Gene breaks out of his narrative of the past in order to describe this, his "moment in history," a time that had imprinted itself forever upon him. The author uses this flashback within a flashback to heighten the contrast between the war-changed outside world and the relative peace of Devon.

Chapter 4: Gene returns to Devon in time to take the test, the first that he has ever failed. That evening, Finny accuses Gene of striving to be head of their class; and Gene admits that he is, realizing for the first time that, if he succeeds, he and Finny will be "even": Finny in athletics and Gene in academics. When Finny states that he would kill himself out of envy if Gene should accomplish his goal, Gene believes him. Carrying the thought of their rivalry further, Gene determines that he and Finny are already "even," in mutual hatred of each other's abilities. He then concludes that Finny's diversionary tactics have been a deliberate attempt to prevent him from achieving his goal of academic excellence. From this point on, Gene considers Finny his enemy but continues to play the role of "best friend" so that Finny won't understand him as well as he understands Finny. As Gene attempts to study for a French examination, Finny interrupts him, insisting that Gene go to the tree. In the ensuing argument between Gene and Finny, Gene realizes with certainty that his assessment of their relationship has been completely inaccurate. There never has been and never could be any rivalry between them. Gene is certain that Finny has never been jealous of him and is a better person than he, admitting also to himself that he cannot bear the thought of this. When they reach the tree, Finny suggests they jump together. While they are on the limb, Gene jounces it, causing Finney to lose his balance and fall on the bank. Gene then jumps from the limb with sureness and without fear for the first time.

Literary Focus: By determining that his "god" Finny is really a "devil" who is deliberately attempting to destroy him, Gene betrays himself as all too human in his readiness to blame his own shortcomings on someone else. Because he cannot and does not perceive the world as Finny does, Gene masks his own feelings of inferiority by his "sighting of the enemy." However, when

he discovers the rivalry is non-existent, Gene savagely fights for self-survival: he denies and betrays this "god"; he attempts to destroy the god, who he wrongly had believed was trying to destory him, and thus free himself of this conflict. The reader is held captive by the narrator here. Gene, unlike Finny, is dishonest. He holds things back, instead of bringing them out in the open. The reader is forced to accept his conclusions about Finny, since there is no other evidence but Gene's. Like him, we feel that it is our understanding that becomes menaced; that we have lost our grasp of the situation. When Gene and Finny are "out on the limb" together, Gene cuts off his thoughts and emotions, describing only the action. The reader is unsure of the truth.

Chapter 5: For several days no one is allowed to visit Finny; the only news is that one of his legs has been shattered. Gene, who feels guilty but hasn't been accused by anyone, spends a great deal of time alone in their room. One evening, after he puts on Finny's clothes, including the pink shirt, he looks into the mirror and sees that he "is" Phineas. The feeling of relief this gives him disappears as soon as he awakens the next morning, when he is once again confronted with what he has done to Finny. Dr. Stanpole informs Gene that Finny's leg is so badly injured that he will never again play sports; he asks Gene to help Finny face that fact and accept it. When Gene visits Finny, the two of them discuss the incident. Gene pretends ignorance of how the accident occurred. Finny does admit that he "had a feeling" about Gene and the accident, one which didn't make any sense and so must be forgotten. After he apologizes to Gene for this, Gene determines that he must confess. However, the doctor comes in before he can do so and Gene is sent away. Soon thereafter, Finny is taken by ambulance to his home.

After a month's vacation, following the end of the Summer Session, Gene returns to Boston and goes to Finny's home. Gene tells Finny that he caused the accident, but Finny can't accept this truth and orders Gene to go away. Realizing that he is hurting Finny again, Gene knows he must deny what he has said. Admitting that he isn't making much sense, Gene takes his leave of Finny, determined he will make it all up to him once Finny returns to Devon.

Literary Focus: Gene's sense of "freedom" is short-lived. Rather than finding an escape from Finny, Gene realizes he wants more than ever to be as much like Finny as possible. The reader should, at this point, make a mental note to determine whether, in the final analysis, Gene accomplishes this desire. The reader should also note that Gene is once again attempting to "find himself," to establish his own values, by following his desire to visit Finny at his home and confess his "sins." During this confession, Gene acknowledges his savagery by asking Finny to hit him or kill him since he knows how it feels to want to destroy something.

Two major conflicts in the novel stem from the relationship between Gene and his roommate Finny, exemplifying both man vs. man (external) and man vs. himself (internal) conflicts. Because Gene determines that he and Finny are "even in enmity," Gene is in conflict with his roommate and his best friend. However, Finny is not really aware that there is a conflict until, much after the fact, he finally faces the truth: that Gene caused him to fall from the tree limb, a fall which has left him unable ever to participate in sports again and has made him ineligible for acceptance into any military service, American or foreign. As a result of his action against Finny, Gene is faced with an ongoing internal struggle in which he tries to determine who he really is by attempting to come to terms with what he did to Finny.

In addition to the conflicts established by the relationship between Gene and Finny, all the students at Devon are faced with a more far-reaching and all-encompassing example of a Man vs. Man conflict: Will they indeed become soldiers in World War II? If so, will they "measure up" to the challenge?

Chapter 6: Upon his return to Devon, Gene realizes that the "gypsy days" of the Summer Session have changed his attitude about Devon. Reporting as assistant senior crew manager for the rowing team, Gene engages in a verbal conflict with Quackenbush, the crew manager, who calls Gene "maimed." Gene attacks Quackenbush and they both land in the river. On his way back to his room, Gene encounters Mr. Ludsbury, who informs him that the laxness of the Summer Session is ended. He chastises Gene and the other "old boys" for taking advantage of the situation. He also informs Gene he has had a long distance phone call. Calling the operator, Gene soon finds himself talking with Finny, who wants to know whom Gene is rooming with. Finny admits he is relieved to learn that Gene hasn't let them put anybody in his place, also admitting he had had a trace of doubt about it since Gene had been "so crazy" at Finny's home. Changing the topic to sports, Finny informs Gene that, since Finny can't play them, Gene must play them for Finny. In spite of Gene's resolve that he would have nothing more to do with sports, he acknowledges

losing part of himself to Finny at that moment and feels his purpose all along has been "to become a part of Phineas."

Literary Focus: Gene is, in a sense, doing penance for his crime against Finny. He has renounced sports for himself and has taken a lowly job as assistant crew manager, a job usually reserved for the physically disabled. In addition, when Gene feels that he fought Quackenbush for Finny, he perhaps realizes that he, like Finny, is also somehow "maimed." When Finny informs Gene he must play sports for him, Gene wonders if his purpose all along hadn't been to "become a part of Phineas." Now that Finny is crippled and will be dependent on Gene in some ways, Gene can become a real part of Finny's life, something he couldn't do while Finny was "whole."

The imagery in Chapter 6 is particularly sharp in pointing out the layers of dualities that exist at Devon. The school is astride two rivers, the upper a clear, refreshing stream, the lower (the Naguamsett) an ugly, salty marsh. Everything at Devon is tormented by its opposite and forced to confront it: studious types vs. athletic types, Rococco architecture vs. Puritan, Army recruiters vs. teaching Masters, and so on. The examples of such opposites, pitted against each other, are numerous.

Chapter 7: Back in his room, Gene's reflection on the phone call is interrupted by a visit from Brinker Hadley, who "jokingly" accuses Gene of having chosen Finny for a roommate, suggesting that somehow Gene knew he'd have the room to himself and that maybe Gene even planned it. Trying to escape Brinker's attack, Gene suggests they go to the Butt Room for a smoke. Once there, Brinker continues his pursuit of the "prisoner," charging Gene with "rankest treachery." Gene deflects the onslaught by reeling off a series of joke "crimes" he has committed against Finny, stopping short of admitting to the one he actually is guilty of. He also diverts Brinker by making one of the younger boys the victim of ridicule. The issue is not raised again, and the boys settle into the routine of studying, club meetings, and sports. In addition, they participate in the war effort in various ways. After spending a day shoveling snow out of the railroad yard, Brinker tells Gene he plans to enlist the following day. Gene contemplates the advantages of such a decision for himself, feeling that it would enable him to close the door on his past and make a clean start. Having decided he will do just that, Gene returns to his room to find that Finny has returned.

Literary Focus: At the mock trial, Brinker calls Gene a prisoner, which indeed he is: Gene is a prisoner inside himself, bearing the full weight of his crime entirely alone. Gene cleverly deflects attention from himself, and the matter is dropped, at least for the time being. The reader should recall Brinker's description of Leper as a "naturalist" in relation to subsequent incidents involving Leper. (He observes events in detail.) Gene believes he has found an escape from his past, but his plan to join the war in which the enemies are clearly defined is curtailed by Finny's return, an example of situational irony.

Chapter 8: The following morning, Brinker enters Gene's room, asking whether Gene is ready to sign up. In the ensuing discussion, Gene realizes that Finny is shocked at the thought of Gene's deserting him, that Finny needs him and wants him around. Responding to Finny's reaction, Gene tells Brinker that enlisting is a "nutty idea," and Finny beams with pleasure. One morning Finny suggests they cut their classes and go to the gym. Finny is annoyed when he discovers that Gene has not gone out for sports. After Gene explains that sports don't seem important with the war going on, Finny launches into his theory that there is no war, that it's only a joke being perpetrated by "fat old men" to protect their jobs. When Gene asks Finny why he gets the joke and the rest of them don't, Finny blurts out that it's because he has suffered. Gene breaks the tension by going to the chinning bar. Both boys are startled by Finny's bitterness.

Finny tells Gene that he had planned to train for the 1944 Olympics but announces that he will train Gene instead. Right before Christmas, Finny's training of Gene pays off when Gene finds his "rhythm" while running. Finny chastises Gene for having been lazy and accuses him of not having known anything about himself. Gene notices a remoteness in Finny and observes that Finny seems older to him and smaller as well. When Mr. Ludsbury, who has been watching Gene exercise, tells the boys to keep in mind that all exercise should be aimed toward preparation for the war, Finny flatly and defiantly tells him, "No."

Literary Focus: Despite his impulsive plan to enlist, it seems that Gene is not yet ready to make a new start. His discovery that Finny needs him, and wants his company, brings back to him the peace of summer that he'd thought was lost. The author uses the imagery of the playing fields crusted under congealed snow to show the dichotomy in Gene's emotions. As the winter term goes on, the two boys tutor each other in their respective specialties. They become even in effort, and Gene finally admits that he had previously not know anything about himself.

Chapter 9: After having seen a war film about the United States ski troops, Leper enlists. This, however, makes the war seem even more unreal to Gene than ever. Brinker unwittingly connects the Devon students to the war by joking that Leper must have been the unknown person in the newspaper article he was reading, who had attempted to kill Hitler. All the boys wonder whether they will measure up in the army, and they hope that the incompetent Leper is the hero they're imagining. Gene has little time to worry about the war because Finny, slowly but surely, creates a world inhabited only by him and Gene, training for the Olympics. On one of many dreary winter days, Finny announces that the following Saturday they need to organize the Devon Winter Carnival. When Gene replies that no such thing exists, Finny replies that it does now. Included in the day's activities are hard cider, games, prizes, a "choreography of peace" performed by Finny, and a Decathlon in which Gene surpasses himself. Gene the adult reflects that the exhilaration all the boys felt came not from the cider but from the "separate peace" they tore from the realities of that gray day in 1943. Their joy and celebration end when Gene receives a telegram from Leper stating that he has "escaped" and needs help.

Literary Focus: Gene has two notions about the war: either it is nonexistent, as Finny asserts, or it is "unreal," since Leper has enlisted. Leper's enlistment does provoke Gene to return to self-examination, causing him to wonder if he has "evolved" as he should have. At the Winter Carnival, Gene is again caught up in Finny's offbeat world. Admitting that he could have done anything Finny had asked him to, Gene is still heavily under Finny's influence.

The arrival of the telegram from Leper causes Gene and Finny to face a reality they have both denied. Chapter 9 brings the concept from which the title is drawn into sharp focus. Gene says that it was the escape they had concocted (the Winter Carnival), this illusory and separate peace, that made him surpass himself. Many conflicting statements about peace have been made in the novel. Is a "separate" peace a contradiction in terms? Gene has also said that peace is indivisible, especially when he is happy within Finny's vision of it. On the first page of the story, he realizes, with surprise, how much fear had pervaded everything during his years at Devon. Could there really have been a special peace within the fear? In the end, the "separate" peace he found was within himself, in his reconciliation of opposing forces within himself, thanks to Finny.

Chapter 10: Traveling toward Leper's home in Vermont, Gene concludes that, since one doesn't "escape" from the army, Leper surely must have escaped from spies. After Gene arrives, Leper explains that he had escaped from the army after all and introduces Gene to a new word: *psycho*. Gene's concern for Leper shifts to fear for himself and the other Devon students who might also soon have to encounter the army. Explaining that the army wanted to give him a Section Eight, Leper says he couldn't accept that since it would mean he could never get a job. In the ensuing conversation, Leper charges Gene with being a "savage underneath" and supports his charge by referring to the "time you knocked Finny out of the tree." Gene kicks Leper's chair over. As Leper laughs and cries, his mother intercedes, asking Gene if he had come there to abuse Leper. Gene apologizes, suggesting he should leave, but Leper asks him to stay for lunch. Gene accepts. Afterward, the two take a walk and Leper recounts the "gory details" of his breakdown. He wonders whether he is psycho or whether the army is, since it turned everything inside out for him. Gene, who has not responded, finally screams at Leper to shut up, that he doesn't want to hear this, that he doesn't care what happened to Leper, that none of it has anything to do with him. Running toward town, Gene leaves Leper "telling his story into the wind."

Literary Focus: Gene makes the trip to visit Leper without Finny and, consequently, is forced to face himself. Gene is uncomfortable and afraid in Leper's presence. Leper's accusation that Gene is a "savage underneath" brings out the savagery once again when Gene kicks Leper's chair over. He stays for lunch, admitting to himself that sometimes one "needs to know the facts," perhaps both about himself and about Leper's experience. However, Gene cannot bear to hear about Leper's experience because he cannot face either himself or the real world yet.

Again, the adult Gene breaks in on the narrative during the student Gene's journey to find Leper. He says that he never really got to the war, that he ended up making endless night trips from one base to the other, as the military tried to figure out what to do with everyone during the last days of the war. It is somewhat anti-climactic; yet at the same time, this revelation sets the tone for a futile endeavor: going to help Leper.

Chapter 11: Returning to Devon, Gene is anxious to see Finny because the only conflict Finny believed existed was between athletes. He brushes aside Finny's inquiry about Leper and joins in a snowball fight with the other boys. Later it occurs to Gene to suggest that Finny perhaps shouldn't get involved in such fights because of his leg.

Finny replies that he is very careful and that he thinks he can feel his leg getting stronger. Brinker comes to their room and pursues the issue of Leper, coming to the correct analysis of Leper's condition on his own, which Gene verifies. A few days later, Brinker confronts Gene about his hesitation to enlist, charging Gene with not doing so because he pities Finny. He goes on to insist that the matter of Finny's accident should be cleared up and forgotten, instilling fear in Gene about what Brinker might eventually say or do. That evening, as Gene helps Finny with a Latin translation, they discuss the war. Finny finally admits that he does believe it is real because he had seen Leper, who must be crazy, hiding in the shrubbery by the chapel.

That night, shortly after 10 P.M., Brinker and three others come for Gene and Finny. Gene believes they are about to participate in some senior prank. However, Brinker's purpose, once they are in the Assembly Room of the First Building, is revealed: they intend to investigate Finny's accident. After interrogating both Gene and Finny, who recite conflicting accounts, someone mentions that Leper had witnessed the accident and would remember exactly what had occurred. Finny quietly reveals that he had seen Leper at Devon that morning. When Brinker sends two boys to find Leper, Gene calculates that no one will believe the testimony of a person "not of sound mind." Leper arrives and gives his account of what he had seen at the tree, but when Brinker asks Leper which of the two boys on the limb moved first, Leper becomes defensive and refuses to say anything more. At this point, Finny rises from his chair, states that he doesn't care and moves toward the doors. Brinker tries to stop him, stating that they don't have all the facts. Finny, crying, shouts back at Brinker to get the rest of the facts, to collect every fact in the world. After hearing Finny's cane tapping on the corridor and the first marble steps, the boys then hear his body falling down the marble stairs.

Literary Focus: Gene's desire to return to Finny's world reflects his need for safety, for an escape from reality. Watching the snowball fight, Gene realizes that Finny thrives on disorder and spontaneity: he can change sides, causing loyalties to be reversed, and still enjoy the game. Just as Gene had turned against Finny, the entire group turns against him in the snowball fight—the only way to end the "confusion" Finny had created. Gene's attempt at living in a fantasy world ends with Finny's admission that there is a war. Finny's fantasy world also crumbles when he is forced to acknowledge that he can trust no one, not even Gene.

Study Guide: A Separate Peace

Throughout the story, Knowles has used "woods" and "the tree" as symbols. Gene often daydreams about the woods beyond the stadium, believing that they reach in unbroken forests all the way to the great Arctic wilderness. He longs to escape to that faraway, untouched grove of pine. Even his last name, Forrester, is connected with trees. Trees seem to represent the solid, solitary growth that he hopes to achieve—a part of his own separate peace.

Chapter 12: As the wrestling coach covers Finny with a blanket, Gene stays out of the way, fearing that Finny will curse him, lose his head completely, and be worse off. After Dr. Stanpole arrives and Finny is carried away on a chair, his eyes shut tight against being an "object of help," Gene realizes that Finny had never thought of Gene's aid as help because Finny had considered Gene an extension of himself. After Finny is taken to the Infirmary, Gene crouches outside the window of Finny's room, and, when everyone has gone, he climbs up to Finny's window and opens it. Finny thrashes wildly in his bed, unable to move because of his leg, and accuses Gene of having come to break something else in him. When Finny half falls out of bed, Gene repeats several times that he is sorry and restrains himself from entering the room to help Finny.

After lying on the ground for awhile, Gene wanders aimlessly about feeling totally isolated from the "meaningful world" around him, and finally spends the night under the stadium. When he returns to his room, he finds a message from Dr. Stanpole asking Gene to bring some things to Finny. As Gene approaches Finny's room, he knows that he must make Finny hear the truth. Gene explains to Finny that he had tried to tell him the truth in Boston and that he had come to the Infirmary the night before because he had felt he belonged there. Finny then admits to Gene that he had been writing letters all winter trying to get acceptance into some service, without any success, and that he could only have admitted there was a war if he knew he could participate. Gene tries to reassure Finny by telling him that injury or no injury, he wouldn't be any good in a war, that he'd get everything so confused he'd make a "terrible mess" of the war. Starting to cry, Finny shifts the conversation to the original accident. He states his belief that surely Gene had done what he did out of some blind impulse, that it hadn't been anything personal. Gene assures Finny he is right but asks how he can ever expect Finny to believe that he had acted out of "some ignorance" inside him. Nodding his head, Finny says that he does understand.

When Gene returns to the Infirmary at 5 P.M., as Dr. Stanpole had instructed him, the doctor tells Gene that Finny is dead. He suspects that some of the bone marrow must have escaped when he was setting Finny's leg, that it must have traveled to his heart and killed him. Gene the adult admits that he did not cry then, or ever, for Finny, not even at the funeral, since he felt that the funeral was his own and that it was not appropriate to cry in such a case.

Literary Focus: Seeing Finny, for the first time totally isolated from all those around him, Gene realizes fully how little he has understood Finny and what a "false" friend he has been to him. When they discuss the accident, Gene reveals his "savagery" to Finny, who accepts his explanation. That he does not cry at Finny's funeral indicates that Gene has finally come to terms with himself—that part of himself that was "savage" is dead and gone.

Finny has now completely fulfilled his Christ-like symbolism. In dying, he frees Gene from his sins. Gene has become absorbed into him, and they are one.

Chapter 13: In June, the Far Common of Devon, which had been donated to the war effort, is occupied by the army. Watching the activity, Gene observes that the summer's peace will surely prevent any serious accomplishment of urgent work. Brinker's father comes to Devon to visit and engages in conversation with Brinker and Gene in the Butt Room. Mr. Hadley gives the two boys a pep talk about the glory of serving one's country and is somewhat annoyed that they don't seem to share his point of view. After he departs, Brinker comments that it is his father's crowd that is responsible for the war but admits that the young ones will have to fight it for them. Gene recalls Finny's "joke" about the fat old men, but reasons that wars aren't caused by generations but by "something ignorant in the human heart." Remembering Finny, Gene acknowledges that, all these years later, he is now able to live in the kind of atmosphere Finny created—a sizing-up of the world with "personal reservations," a sifting through of its "rocklike facts," and an acceptance of only what he "could assimilate without a sense of chaos and loss." Only Finny, states Gene, had escaped finding himself pitted against something in the world that overwhelmed him and which had ultimately broken the simplicity and unity of his character. Since Finny had escaped this, unlike all others Gene ever knew, Gene admits he had broken Finny's "harmonious and natural unity."

As he prepares to leave Devon, Gene feels he is ready for the war now that he has no hatred to contribute to it, stating that his fury is gone, absorbed by Finny and taken from him. Reflecting then on his time in the service, the adult Gene states that he never killed anyone in the war and that he never felt hatred for the enemy because he had killed his enemy while he had been on active duty at school. He goes on to state that only Finny had never been afraid and had never hated anyone. All others created an enemy and constructed lines of defense against this enemy at great cost to themselves—an enemy who may not have been an enemy at all.

Literary Focus: In the final analysis, Gene has, at least in part, become Finny. His approach to life has become what Finny's had been, in that he rejects certain things he can't accept and can now exist "without a sense of chaos and loss." Gene knows that, just as "grownups" create enemies, he had created an enemy in Finny, one that had never existed. He understands that he had killed his enemy at school. Perhaps he believes he did kill Finny, but he also knows that he conquered and killed the savagery within himself. The author in completing the frame of the story, eloquently illustrates Gene's victorious completion of the journey into himself.

Reading Guide Questions

Responding to the Novel

Analyzing the Novel

Chapter 1
Identifying Facts

1. Looking at the stairs in the First Academy Building, what surprising fact does the narrator (identified in Chapter 5 as Gene Forrester) realize he had overlooked about them?
2. When Gene visits the tree, what does it resemble?
3. How does Gene feel about having seen the tree? Why?
4. To what time does the story flash back?
5. Who of the five boys is eager to jump from the tree?
6. Describe the relationship between the narrator (Gene) and Phineas (Finny).

Interpreting Meanings

7. Why, after fifteen years, do you think Gene returned to Devon School? Why do you think he is upset that the school looks like a "museum"? Why wouldn't he want it to?
8. Gene states that the two places he wanted to see at Devon School were "fearful sites." Why does he use this term? What is fearful about marble stairs? about a tree? If they are "fearful," why do you think Gene wants to see them?
9. Gene explains that the Summer Session the boys were attending was established to keep up with the pace of the war. He states that the seniors were being trained for the war and were "practically soldiers." What effect might the war have on the "Upper Middlers" (the juniors) like Gene and Finny?
10. Why must Gene, against his better judgment, jump from the tree? How does this and his later "wrestling match" with Finny affect their relationship? What does this tell you about the personalities of the two?

Chapter 2
Identifying Facts

1. Why does Phineas decide he will wear his pink shirt?
2. What is Gene beginning to realize about Phineas? What is Gene's reaction to this realization?
3. What does Phineas wear as a belt at the traditional tea? Explain why he does this.
4. What club do Phineas and Gene form?
5. When Gene and Finny are on the tree limb together, what happens? What does Gene later realize?

Interpreting Meanings

6. Gene states that one of Finny's reasons for living was "a flow of simple, unregulated friendliness" between people. What does Gene mean? Do you think this is a good "reason for living"?
7. Gene states that the faculty of the school "loosened its grip" on the boys partly because of Finny and partly because the boys reminded them of "what peace was like." Is the faculty's reaction believable? Why would the authority figures be likely to be more lenient than usual in this situation?
8. Gene admits that he is envious of Finny, who could get away with anything. He states that there's no harm in envying a best friend a little. Do you agree with Gene or not? Explain.
9. When Finny insists they jump from the tree again, why do you think Gene agrees to it, even though he is obviously afraid to do so? Is Gene's reaction to "peer pressure" a typical one?

Chapter 3
Identifying Facts

1. How do Gene and Finny open every meeting of their SSS of the SS? How does Gene feel about this?
2. Why does Finny invent "blitzball"?
3. After Finny breaks a swimming record, what does he make Gene promise?
4. Explain why Gene is shocked about Finny's decision. What does it make him feel about Finny?

5. What "courageous" thing does Finny admit to Gene before they go to sleep on the beach? What is Gene's response? Why?

Interpreting Meanings

6. Gene has conflicting emotions about Finny having "practically saved his life" because it was Finny's fault he had "practically lost" it. Yet Gene continues to go to the nightly meetings and jump from the tree without protest. Why do you think he does this?

7. Later in the chapter, Gene states that Finny could "shine" at many things besides "blitzball," such as getting along with everyone. Gene states that he is glad of that because Finny is his roommate and best friend. Is Gene really glad? What do you think he might really be feeling? Recall Gene's earlier statement about it being all right to envy one's best friend a little. Is Gene envying Finny more and more?

8. After Finny states that Gene is his "best pal," Gene isn't able to return the compliment. He states that he perhaps was "stopped by that level of feeling, deeper than thought, which contains the truth." What "truth" do you think Gene is feeling? Why?

Chapter 4
Identifying Facts

1. What does Finny accuse Gene of striving for?

2. What does Gene realize his being head of the class would mean?

3. When Finny says he would kill himself "out of jealous envy," what is Gene's reaction?

4. What does Gene determine that he and Finny are even in? Why?

5. What second realization does Gene have about Finny?

6. Describe the effect Gene's second realization has on his efforts as a student.

7. Why does Gene continue to attend the meetings of the Suicide Society?

8. Before they reach the tree, what does Gene realize about the rivalry between him and Finny? How does he feel about this?

9. Describe what Gene does while he and Finny are on the limb together.

10. How is Gene's jump from the limb different from all his others?

Interpreting Meanings

11. Finny tells Gene he would be so jealous, if Gene became head of their class, that he'd kill himself out of envy. Gene believes Finny is telling the truth, that Finny's joking manner is a screen. What other reaction could Gene have had? Why do you think he chose to react in this manner?

12. Gene determines that Finny had deliberately set out to wreck Gene's grades with all his diversions. He blames Finny totally. Is Gene being realistic? Does Gene have any responsibility for his own actions? How is Gene's behavior here typical of human nature?

13. After Gene jounces the limb, he hears Finny hit the bank with a thud. Why do you think Gene jounced the limb? Was his action premeditated? What were his thoughts about himself and Finny just prior to the jump? Gene then jumps from the limb for the first time without fear. What explanation can you offer for this?

Chapter 5
Identifying Facts

1. What fact emerges about Finny's condition?

2. Describe how Gene feels when he puts on Finny's pink shirt.

3. What does Dr. Stanpole tell Gene about Finny and sports?

4. What does Finny apologize to Gene for?

5. Explain why Gene doesn't tell Finny what he intended to tell him.

6. Describe Finny's response when Gene admits he caused Finny's accident.

7. What does Gene realize he is doing to Finny by admitting the truth? What does he then know he must do?

8. What does Gene determine he will do when Finny returns to Devon?

Interpreting Meanings

9. Gene admits that if anyone had been suspicious of what he had done to Finny he might have developed some defense of himself. What does Gene mean? Why would having been accused be easier to deal with?

10. Gene wants to tell Finny the truth about what happened and begins to do so. Why is it important for him to tell the truth? Who will it help more, him or Finny? Why?

11. Even when Gene tells Finny the truth, that he caused Finny to fall, Finny is unable to

believe it and denies it. Why does he react this way? Why do you think he cannot believe the truth even when he hears it?

Chapter 6
Identifying Facts

1. What does Gene conclude is the point of the sermon he hears upon his return to Devon?
2. Why does Gene hit Quackenbush?
3. Why is Finny relieved to find that he and Gene will still be roommates?
4. What directive does Finny give Gene about playing sports?
5. After hearing Finny's directive to him, what does Gene then feel his (Gene's) purpose must have been?

Interpreting Meanings

6. Gene indicates his regret at not having "seized and held and prized the multitudes of advantages" the summer had offered him. What advantages had the summer offered? What hadn't he prized?
7. During his phone call to Gene, Finny again apologizes to Gene for having had doubts about him. Finny outwardly refuses to accept the truth about what Gene has done to him. Of what, then, might these "doubts" be an indication?
8. Gene states that he "lost part of myself" to Finny and realizes that his purpose had been "to become a part of Phineas." What do you think Gene means by this? Why would he want or need to become a part of Finny?

Chapter 7
Identifying Facts

1. What does Brinker accuse Gene of having done in regard to choosing Finny as a roommate?
2. Describe how Gene manages to maintain control when he is "accused" in the Butt Room.
3. When Gene is recounting the series of "crimes" he had committed against Finny, what words could he not say?
4. How does Gene shift the attention from himself?
5. What does Leper do while the other boys aid in the "war effort"?
6. What is Gene's reaction to Brinker's announcement that he will enlist the following day? What decision does Gene make?

7. What effect does Finny's return have on Gene's plans?

Interpreting Meanings

8. Why do you think Gene is unable to say he had pushed Finny out of the tree? What had he promised himself he would do when Finny returned to Devon? What effect might his admission to the other boys of what he had done have on the relationship between him and Finny?
9. Gene admits that there was always "something deadly" in the things he wanted or loved, and that if it wasn't there, he put it there himself, as he had done with Finny. What is Gene saying? What is he acknowledging about himself?
10. Near the end of the chapter, Gene states that the war was chipping away at the one thing he had loved at Devon, "the measureless, careless peace of the Devon summer." In view of Gene's jealousy of Finny and his causing Finny to fall, had it been a careless, peaceful summer? Recall his earlier comment, in Chapter 6, that he hadn't taken advantage of the situation the summer had offered him. How do you account for these differing conclusions?

Chapter 8
Identifying Facts

1. Why does Gene feel a certain "disapproval" of Finny?
2. What does Gene realize about Finny's reaction to the thought of his enlisting?
3. Why does Gene feel that peace has come back to Devon for him?
4. Summarize Finny's conclusion about the war.
5. Why does Finny say he understands the joke about the war?
6. What are both Gene and Finny startled by? What do the boys do about this discovery?
7. Describe the plan Finny announces he has for Gene.
8. After Gene finds his rhythm, what does Finny tell him?
9. What does Mr. Ludsbury tell Finny about exercise? What is Finny's response?

Interpreting Meanings

10. Gene observes that prior to Finny's return, he had felt that each new day erased past

Study Guide: A Separate Peace

failures and opened all possibilities anew. Now, in the winter of snow and crutches, he feels that "each morning reasserted the problems of the night before, that sleep suspended all but changed nothing." Which description is closer to *your* feelings about morning? Discuss a time in your life that illustrates your position.

11. Before Finny's return to Devon, Gene had looked forward to enlisting and making a clean start. When he realizes that Finny needs him, even though he has been untrustworthy, Gene decides to stay at Devon. Why do you think he makes this decision? What motivates him to give up his plan to make a clean start? Do you think Finny needs Gene? If so, why?

12. Finny tells Gene that "when you really love something, then it loves you back, in whatever way it has to love." Gene doesn't think this is true. What do you think?

Chapter 9
Identifying Facts

1. What does Leper's enlistment make Gene feel about the war?

2. What conclusion does Leper come to about "everything" after seeing the war film?

3. As the boys joke about Leper's "glories," what do they wonder about themselves and what do they hope about Leper?

4. Describe the type of "world" Finny eventually creates for himself and Gene.

5. Explain how Gene convinces Brinker to go along with the Winter Carnival.

6. Describe how Finny opens the Games of the Winter Carnival.

7. What does Gene say Finny's "dance" was?

8. To what does Gene attribute his surpassing himself in the Decathlon?

9. What occurs that causes the "special and separate" peace of that afternoon to drain away?

Interpreting Meanings

10. Gene states that the film about the United States ski troops revealed what they all were seeking: "a recognizable and friendly face to the war." He goes on to say it "was the cleanest image of war" that he had ever seen. Why were the boys seeking a "friendly face to the war"? What images of war does one usually have?

11. Leper concludes that "Everything has to

evolve or else it perishes." Gene asks himself how Leper's theory applies to him, to Phineas, and to Leper. Why do you think Gene is wondering about this? How do you think Leper's theory might apply to each of the three boys?

12. Leper signs the telegram he sends to Gene, "Your best friend." Why do you think Leper does this? Has there been any indication that Gene is Leper's friend, particularly a best friend?

Chapter 10
Identifying Facts

1. What does the "older" narrator reveal about his army career?

2. What conclusion does Gene come to about Leper's "escape"?

3. Why does Gene react with fear to Leper's use of the word *psycho?*

4. When Leper accuses Gene of being a "savage underneath," what example does he use to make his point?

5. For what two reasons does Gene accept Leper's invitation to stay for lunch?

6. Explain why Leper thinks maybe it is the army that is psycho.

7. Describe how Gene reacts to the "gory details" of Leper's story.

8. Why does Gene say he doesn't care about what happened to Leper?

Interpreting Meanings

9. Before Gene reaches Leper's house, he is encouraged by his fantasy that Leper had escaped from spies, that "this wasn't going to be such a bad war," after all. What do you think he means? Why would he want to believe this?

10. By the end of lunch, Gene is certain that Leper's mother is convinced Gene is "a good boy underneath." Gene states that Leper was "closer to the truth" (when he said Gene was a "savage underneath"). What is your opinion of Gene? Is he a "good boy" or is he a "savage"?

11. Gene tells Leper that he doesn't care what happened to him because it has nothing to do with him. Why do you think Gene reacts so violently to what Leper is relating to him? Do you think he really doesn't care? Does it really have nothing to do with him?

Chapter 11
Identifying Facts

1. Why does Gene want to see only Phineas when he returns to Devon?
2. What happens during the snowball fight?
3. Describe Brinker's reaction when he finds out what happened to Leper.
4. Why does Brinker believe Gene has put off enlisting? How does Brinker say Finny should be treated? Why?
5. What does Brinker say should be done about Finny's accident?
6. What does Finny say convinced him the war was real?
7. When Brinker and his friends come for Gene and Finny, what does Gene think is happening?
8. What does Brinker say they have convened to do?
9. When Brinker sends two boys to bring Leper to the Assembly Room, what calculations does Gene make?
10. After Leper refuses to say anything more, what does Finny tell the group of boys? What does he tell Brinker in particular?
11. What final sound does the group of boys hear?

Interpreting Meanings

12. When Gene and Finny are discussing Caesar, Finny tells Gene he doesn't believe books and teachers but that he does believe Gene, and that he knows Gene better than anybody. Why does Finny need to believe Gene? Does he really know Gene?
13. Brinker tells the group that for both Finny and Gene's good, the matter of Finny's accident should be brought out into the open. He then tells Finny they aren't trying to make him feel bad. What do you think is Brinker's motivation for imagining himself, as Gene puts it, "Justice incarnate"? Why is he so determined to force this issue? Isn't it likely that Finny will be made to feel bad, considering the subject of discussion? Is Brinker, in your opinion, trying to help anyone? If so, whom?
14. At the end of Leper's testimony, Finny calls out, "I just don't care. Never mind." What do you think he means? If he doesn't care about the investigation or getting to the "truth," why do you think he mentioned that Leper was at Devon?

Chapter 12
Identifying Facts

1. Why does Gene keep "out of the way" when Phil Latham wraps the blanket around Finny?
2. What realization does Gene have about Finny's lack of pride in accepting Gene's help?
3. What is Dr. Stanpole's diagnosis of Finny's condition?
4. When Finny discovers Gene at the window, what does he accuse Gene of?
5. When Gene takes Finny's suitcase to the Infirmary, what does Finny admit he has been doing all winter? What has been the result?
6. What does Gene tell Finny about his being in the war?
7. What explanation does Gene give Finny about what he had done in the tree? What does Finny tell Gene?
8. What does Dr. Stanpole conclude was the cause of Finny's death?
9. Why does Gene say he didn't ever cry about Finny?

Interpreting Meanings

10. As Gene watches Finny being carried out in the chair, he states that he again had the feeling "of having all along ignored what was finest" in Finny. What do you think Gene was referring to? What, in your opinion, was "finest" in Finny?
11. Gene tells Finny that what he did to him wasn't "anything personal," that it was just "some ignorance inside" him, "something blind." Is Gene telling Finny the truth? Recall Gene's realization right before the jump that there hadn't, after all, been any rivalry between him and Finny.
12. Gene the adult states that he had never cried about Finny, that at Finny's funeral he had had a feeling it had been his own. What do you think Gene means? Recall his earlier remark that his purpose had been to become part of Finny.

Chapter 13
Identifying Facts

1. Who occupies the Far Common? What do they bring with them?
2. Why does Gene conclude that none of the Devon boys ever accused him of being responsible for what had happened to Finny?

3. What does Brinker's father tell Gene and Brinker?

4. Restate the conclusion Gene comes to about the cause of wars.

5. What, according to Gene, had Phineas alone escaped? Who, then, had inflicted this on Finny?

6. What does Gene say had happened to his fury?

7. Explain why Gene says his war ended before he ever put on a uniform?

8. Describe what, according to Gene, people who ''sight'' the enemy do.

9. Who constructed lines against their enemies, and at what cost? What does Gene wonder about ''this enemy''?

Interpreting Meanings

10. Mr. Hadley tells Gene and Brinker that one's greatest moment, greatest privilege, is to serve one's country. He goes on to say that the ''old guys'' like him are proud of the young ones going off to war, and jealous of them, too. Brinker then angrily tells Gene that the ''old guys'' are responsible for the war but that the young ones will have to fight it. Comment on these two divergent opinions about war. Do you think they are typical of all the older and younger generations?

11. Gene states that everyone he ever knew, except for Finny, found themselves ''pitted violently against something in the world around them,'' and that this ''hostile thing'' broke ''the simplicity and unity of their characters.'' What kinds of ''hostile things'' do people find themselves pitted against? Is Gene just referring to such things as war, or is he perhaps referring to other types of conflict that cause people to change?

12. Gene comments that he was ready for the war since he no longer had any hatred to contribute to it. What does he mean by this?

13. From Gene's experience with his own ''enemy,'' what conclusions does he come to about enemies in general? What do you think Gene is suggesting about human nature in the last paragraph of the novel?

The Novel as a Whole

1. A **protagonist** is defined as the main character in a short story, play, or novel. Discuss Gene Forrester as the protagonist of *A Separate Peace*.

2. An **antagonist** is the adversary who opposes the protagonist. The antagonist may be another character, the forces of nature, fate, or chance, or any combination of these. Discuss Finny as Gene's antagonist. What other antagonists does Gene face in the novel? Defend your choices with evidence from the novel.

3. Although Leper is a relatively minor **character** in the novel, his actions have an impact on both Gene and Finny. Discuss Leper as a *catalyst*—that is, something that effects a change—with regard to these two characters.

4. Brinker's father, Mr. Hadley, appears only briefly in the last chapter of the novel. What is his function with regard to the **plot**?

5. A premeditated act is one which is considered or planned in advance. Was Gene's act of causing Finny to fall from the tree premeditated? Explain your reasoning.

6. Briefly discuss the impact World War II has on Gene, Finny, Leper, and Brinker.

7. The **setting** of a work includes the time and place in which the action occurs. It may simply serve as a background for characters and events or it may help to create the atmosphere from which the story evolves. Setting may directly affect the plot's development and may aid in the understanding of character—even be vital to that understanding. Evaluate the function of the setting, including both time and place, of *A Separate Peace*, and analyze how the setting furthers the plot's development and the development of the characters.

8. Although Knowles doesn't clearly specify what he intends the tree to symbolize, it is obvious that it is a **symbol.** Based on your understanding of the novel, what possible interpretations can you suggest?

9. Some works have more than one **theme.** Write down a list of the themes you found in *A Separate Peace*. Discuss your interpretation of the message(s) you believe Knowles is trying to convey to his readers.

Writing About the Novel

A Creative Response

1. **Creating an Alternate Ending.** Assume that Knowles does not have Finny die at the end of Chapter 12. Write a synopsis of what you think would have happened to the relationship between Gene and Finny after Finny is released from the Infirmary. Remember that Gene has confessed his guilt and Finny has accepted his apology.

2. **Extending a Characterization.** One of Finny's greatest pleasures in life has been his participation in, and excellence at, sports. Imagine that Finny does not die at the end of Chapter 12. Write a synopsis of what you think Finny would have done with his life after he graduated from Devon. Remember that Finny was not a scholar but that he was from a wealthy Bostonian family.

3. **Writing a Flashback.** Imagine that the story was not told by the narrator from a distance of fifteen years after the facts, but by a young Gene. Write a synopsis of Gene's feelings about Finny and his experiences at Devon if the story had been written when Gene was eighteen or nineteen. In other words, replace the content of Knowles's Chapter 13 by using Gene's perspective only a year or two after his graduation.

A Critical Response

4. **Responding to a Critic.** One critic stated in his review of *A Separate Peace* that, "Finny is never completely credible [as a real person]." Defend or refute this statement, using evidence from the novel.

5. **Evaluating a Title.** The title Knowles gives his novel comes from the end of Chapter 9, where Gene discusses the Devon Winter Carnival and states that the exhilaration the boys felt came from "this liberation we had torn from the gray encroachments of 1943, the escape we had concocted, this afternoon of momentary, illusory, special and separate peace." In view of the brevity of the incident of the carnival and its relative importance compared to other events of the novel, defend or refute Knowles's choice of this title as the most appropriate one for the novel.

6. **Comparing the Contrasting Characters.** Compare and contrast the personalities of Leper and Brinker. Are they **symbolic** characters? If so, what might they symbolize? Are they, like Gene and Finny, opposites? If so, how is their relationship like Gene and Finny's? How is it different?

7. **Analyzing Characters in Terms of Plot Function.** Discuss the functions of the minor characters Mr. Prud'homme and Mr. Ludsbury in the novel.

8. **Examining Structural Style.** Knowles has stated that the structure of *A Separate Peace* "is linear, a narrative involving two and then four interrelating characters." Discuss the novel's structure in terms of this description.

9. **Analyzing Language.** A reviewer at the *San Francisco Chronicle* said that this book is ". . . a beautifully written story. For style and imagery, *A Separate Peace* ranks with the work of the very best young American novelists. . . ." Analyze Knowles's use of language in the novel. How do the **imagery** and **figures of speech** contribute to the exposition of the themes?

Going Beyond the Novel

A Creative Response

1. **Writing a Letter of Support or Refutation.** You have just read a critical analysis of *A Separate Peace* in which a critic states that, while the novel is, indeed, a good "story," it should only be read by teenage boys who attend private prep schools since they are the only ones who will fully understand what the book is about. Write a letter to the critic in which you defend or refute his claim about the book's audience. Whichever position you take, use specific references to the novel to support your assertions.

2. **Writing a Letter to a Classmate.** You are Brinker. Two years have passed since you and Gene Forrester left Devon School. In that time, you have often thought of your determination to expose the truth of Finny's fall from the tree and his subsequent second injury and death. Write a letter to Gene in which you express your feelings about what you did to Gene and about Finny's death.

3. **Writing a Diary Entry.** You are Leper. A year has passed since your "escape" from the army. Write a diary entry in which you discuss what has happened to you in that year.

4. **Writing a Letter of Recommendation.** After reading *A Separate Peace*, you have given considerable thought to Gene's conclusion that "wars were . . . made by something ignorant in the human heart." You have decided that you agree with Gene and feel that others should read the novel for its anti-war sentiment. Decide who you think would benefit from reading the book and write a letter to him or her in which you recommend *A Separate Peace*. Be sure to give your reader specific reasons why you think he or she should read the book, and support your argument by using specific references to the novel. Since the person hasn't read the book and you want him or her to do so, you must avoid recounting the plot of the story. You will instead tell *about* certain aspects of the story, using those details that will entice the reader to follow your suggestion without giving away the plot of the story.

5. **Writing a Letter of Resignation.** You are Dr. Stanpole and have just attended Finny's funeral. Although you know you did the best that you could for Finny, you feel terribly guilty about this young man's untimely death. Write a letter to the Board of Trustees of Devon School in which you resign as school physician, carefully and clearly explaining to them why you have made this decision.

6. **Writing a Letter of Acceptance or Refusal.** You are the president of the Devon School Board of Trustees. You and the Board members have received Dr. Stanpole's letter of resignation and have discussed it thoroughly among yourselves. Write a letter to Dr. Stanpole in which you give him the Board's decision, either that you accept his resignation or that you refuse it. Whichever position you take, be sure that you clearly explain to Dr. Stanpole the reasons for the Board's decision.

7. **Writing a Letter of Apology.** You are Gene, and having finally graduated from Devon, you are ready to begin active service in the Navy. You have not seen or talked to Leper since the "trial" at which he testified about Finny's fall from the tree. Since your visit to Leper's home, where you told him you didn't want to hear about his experiences in the army and that you didn't care, you have done a great deal of thinking and maturing. Write a letter to Leper in which you discuss your behavior that afternoon and explain why you behaved the way you did.

8. **Writing an Obituary.** You are Finny's father. Write an obituary for Phineas (make up a last name since the author never gives him one) which you will submit to the *Boston Bugle*.

9. **Writing a Poem.** Write your own poem in which you express your feelings about one of the ideas presented in *A Separate Peace*, such as war, peace, friendship, jealousy, loyalty, rivalry, self-identity, or growth.

10. **Writing a Letter of Opinion.** You have read that John Knowles once stated, "The ultimate importance of *A Separate Peace* is that it has reached out to the readers who need it." Write a letter to Mr. Knowles in which you express your opinion of the novel's importance, both to you and to others who might read it. Be sure to use specific references to the novel so that Mr. Knowles will know you are an informed correspondent.

A Critical Response

1. **Comparing and Contrasting Novels.** Read J. D. Salinger's *The Catcher in the Rye*. Compare and contrast the characters Holden Caufield and Gene Forrester.

2. **Researching an Event.** Research the cancellation of the 1944 Olympics.

3. **Researching a Prep School.** Research another preparatory school, such as England's famous Eton or an American military academy (West Point, Annapolis, the Air Force Academy, or the Coast Guard Academy), focusing on its origin, its history, its curriculum, and its goals.

4. **Researching an Award.** Research the William Faulkner Foundation Award. In your report, include a timeline or a chart showing the recipients of the Award from its inception to the present.

5. **Comparing Literature and Film.** View the 1972 film version of *A Separate Peace*. Compare and contrast it with the novel, noting especially ways in which they differ.

6. **Comparing Friendships.** Read Hermann Hesse's novel *Narcissus and Goldmund*. Compare and contrast the friendship of the two main characters with that of Gene and Finny.

7. **Comparing and Contrasting Novels.** Read *The Paragon*, another novel by John Knowles. Compare and contrast it with *A Separate Peace*, with regard to major characters, setting, and theme(s).

8. **Researching a Historical Figure.** Research the life of one of the following persons referred to in the novel. Include information about this person's connection to, or importance in, World War II: Betty Grable, Franklin Delano Roosevelt, General MacArthur, Madame Chiang Kai-shek, Mahatma Gandhi, Winston Churchill, or General de Gaulle.

9. **Researching a Location.** Research one of the following geographical locations or scientific phenomena referred to in the novel: the Northern Lights, Gibraltar, the Gulf Stream, the Polar Ice Cap, or Mount Katahdin.

10. **Researching an Author.** Research the life, and literary career, of one of the following authors referred to in the novel: Virgil, Thomas Hardy, Homer (author of the *Odyssey*), Voltaire, Julius Caesar, Moliere, or Arthur Conan Doyle (author of the Sherlock Holmes mysteries).

11. **Reading and Analyzing a Poem.** Read A. E. Housman's poem, "To an Athlete Dying Young." In one paragraph, summarize the idea expressed in the poem. Then, in a second paragraph, discuss whether you think this poem could be applied to Finny.

12. **Reading from the Old Testament.** Read the story of Phineas in the Old Testament. Summarize it in your own words. Then discuss both the similarities and differences you discover between the biblical Phineas and the fictional Finny. Why do you think John Knowles chose the name "Phineas" for his character?

Testing on the Novel

Developing Vocabulary A

Directions: Write the letter of the definition in the right-hand column that best matches each word in the left-hand column. (*5 points each*)

_____ 1. vindicated	**a.** enraged
_____ 2. treachery	**b.** freed; delivered from
_____ 3. anarchy	**c.** a play on words
_____ 4. reprimand	**d.** argumentative
_____ 5. irate	**e.** the betrayal of trust
_____ 6. insidious	**f.** mutual hostility
_____ 7. rhetorically	**g.** to conclude by reasoning from evidence
_____ 8. resonant	**h.** yielding to wishes
_____ 9. collaborator	**i.** deep and full in sound
_____10. infer	**j.** one who cooperates with an enemy
_____11. indulgent	**k.** in a manner not evoking a reply
_____12. pun	**l.** open to attack
_____13. contentious	**m.** a severe or formal rebuke
_____14. vulnerable	**n.** having no government or law
_____15. enmity	**o.** treacherous but enticing
_____16. opulent	**p.** easily deceived
_____17. pungent	**q.** luxurious; rich
_____18. accolade	**r.** that which touches the feelings deeply
_____19. poignance	**s.** an acknowledgment
_____20. gullible	**t.** sharp or biting

Testing on the Novel

Developing Vocabulary B

Directions: Write the letter of the definition in the right-hand column that best matches each word in the left-hand column. (*5 points each*)

_____ **1.** inveigle

_____ **2.** eloquence

_____ **3.** inane

_____ **4.** candid

_____ **5.** ludicrous

_____ **6.** erratic

_____ **7.** tacit

_____ **8.** venerable

_____ **9.** idiosyncratic

_____ **10.** inured

_____ **11.** essence

_____ **12.** consternation

_____ **13.** incredulously

_____ **14.** parody

_____ **15.** conniver

_____ **16.** cacophony

_____ **17.** austerity

_____ **18.** parry

_____ **19.** aphorisms

_____ **20.** cranium

a. the basic quality of something

b. frank; without deception

c. fluent, forceful speech

d. absurdly amusing

e. a feeble imitation

f. respected because of age

g. accustomed to by experience

h. sudden amazement or dread

i. one who willfully aids wrongdoing

j. to lure by artful talk

k. inconsistent; irregular

l. unbelievingly; skeptically

m. peculiarly individualistic

n. lacking sense or ideas; empty; void

o. understood without being spoken

p. somberness; sternness

q. part of the skull that encloses the brain

r. concise statements of principles

s. to ward off a blow

t. discordant sound

Testing on the Novel

Developing Vocabulary C

Directions: Circle the letter of the best definition for each vocabulary word. (*4 points each*)

1. incongruity

    a. incompatible

    b. inaccurate

    c. indecent

    d. intelligent

2. opulent

    a. obese

    b. luxurious

    c. a precious gem

    d. a type of blood

3. impinge

    a. satisfy

    b. encroach

    c. endanger

    d. enable

4. vagaries

    a. wanderers

    b. unnoticed events

    c. riches

    d. unpredictable actions

5. abashed

    a. injured

    b. elated

    c. embarrassed

    d. employed

6. foreboding

    a. an omen; a feeling of coming doom

    b. a golf term

    c. part of the arm

    d. an accomplishment

7. torpidly

    a. enthusiastically

    b. unhappily

    c. uncertainly

    d. apathetically

8. languid

    a. a pool of water

    b. a skin salve

    c. weak from exhaustion

    d. wealthy

9. futility

    a. uselessness

    b. angriness

    c. anxiousness

    d. fullness

10. bellicose

    a. unconscious

    b. believable

    c. belligerent

    d. betrayal

11. sanctity

    a. holiness

    b. haughtiness

    c. ridiculousness

    d. deliberateness

12. judiciously

    a. with a panel

    b. without thought

    c. without caring

    d. with wisdom

13. discernible

    a. uncomplicated

    b. detectible

    c. upsetting

    d. illegible

14. precariously

    a. unhappily

    b. unclearly

    c. uncertainly

    d. undecidedly

Study Guide: A Separate Peace

15. liaison

    a. a flower wreath

    b. a close bond

    c. a foreign spy

    d. a withdrawal

16. holocaust

    a. devastation

    b. excitement

    c. a religious fanatic

    d. a laser image

17. bane

    a. something harmful

    b. something hard

    c. something imagined

    d. something precious

18. ambiguously

    a. obscurely

    b. honestly

    c. openly

    d. offensively

19. ruefully

    a. responsibly

    b. remarkably

    c. repeatedly

    d. regretfully

20. refuting

    a. agreeing

    b. disproving

    c. replying

    d. ignoring

21. imperceptibly

    a. blatantly

    b. slightly

    c. simply

    d. singularly

22. preeminently

    a. noiselessly

    b. plentifully

    c. predictably

    d. supremely

23. elite

    a. small

    b. simple

    c. superior

    d. incredible

24. urbane

    a. destructive

    b. helpful

    c. polite; polished

    d. rural

25. latent

    a. dormant

    b. impatient

    c. rubberized

    d. printed

● Testing on the Novel

Understanding What Happened/Recognizing Elements of the Novel

A. *Directions:* In each blank, write **T** if the statement is true; write **F** if it is false. (*2 points each*)

_____ 1. The two places the narrator (Gene) wants to see at Devon are the marble stairs in the First Academy Building and the tree.

_____ 2. The story flashes back to the summer of 1912.

_____ 3. Gene starts to realize Finny can get away with anything and admits he is a little envious.

_____ 4. When Finny breaks the school swimming record, he makes Gene promise to tell the swimming coach.

_____ 5. Gene determines that Finny and he are even in their mutual hatred of each other's accomplishments.

_____ 6. When Gene and Finny are on the tree limb together, Gene pushes Finny out of the tree.

_____ 7. Dr. Stanpole tells Gene that Finny may be able to play sports again but that his recovery will take years.

_____ 8. When Gene visits Finny at his home in Boston, he wants to tell Finny the truth about the accident but he doesn't.

_____ 9. Finny determines that Gene will have to play sports for him.

_____ 10. Before Finny returns to Devon, Gene decides that he will enlist in the service.

_____ 11. Brinker accuses Gene of having chosen Finny as his roommate so he'd have their room to himself.

_____ 12. Upon Finny's return he tells Gene there is no war, that it's only a joke made up by fat old men to protect their jobs.

_____ 13. Finny informs Gene he is going to train him for the 1944 Olympics.

_____ 14. After seeing a war film about ski troops, Leper enlists in the army.

_____ 15. Finny organizes the Devon Winter Carnival as a protest against winter, which he hates.

_____ 16. Gene believes he won the Decathlon because of the hard cider he had been drinking.

_____ 17. On his way to Leper's home, Gene convinces himself that Leper has escaped from spies.

_____ 18. Leper accuses Gene of always having been a savage underneath.

_____ 19. Gene confesses to Leper that he had made Finny fall from the tree.

_____ 20. When Leper tells Gene his experiences in the army, Gene tries to comfort him, telling Leper he cares and he understands.

_____ 21. At the First Academy Building, Brinker holds an investigation of Finny's accident.

_____ 22. Leper testifies at the investigation that he doesn't remember anything about Finny's accident.

_____ 23. When Gene takes Finny's suitcase to the Infirmary, Finny says he knows Gene caused the first accident and that he can never forgive him.

_____ 24. Dr. Stanpole tells Gene that Finny died from blood poisoning.

_____ 25. Gene admits that he cried uncontrollably at Finny's funeral.

_____ 26. After the funeral, Brinker and several others accuse Gene of having been responsible for what happened to Finny.

_____ 27. Gene concludes that wars are caused by something ignorant in the human heart.

_____ 28. Gene is anxious to get into the war so he can release the fury and the hatred he feels.

_____ 29. Gene states that he had killed his enemy at school.

_____ 30. Gene says that Finny was the only person he had ever known who hadn't ever been afraid and who hadn't ever hated anyone.

B. *Directions:* Write the letter of the description in the right-hand column that best matches each character in the left-hand column. (*2 points each*)

_____ 31. Brinker

_____ 32. Leper

_____ 33. Finny

_____ 34. Mr. Prud'homme

_____ 35. Gene

_____ 36. Mr. Hadley

_____ 37. Dr. Stanpole

_____ 38. Mr. Ludsbury

_____ 39. Phil Latham

_____ 40. Quackenbush

a. called Gene "maimed"

b. covered Finny with a blanket (was the wrestling coach)

c. was proud of his military record

d. escaped from the army

e. relaxed Devon's standards

f. was too thin to get the joke about the war

g. danced a choreography of peace

h. wanted to be head of his class

i. accused Gene of treachery

j. appealed to Gene to help Finny

C. *Directions:* Write the letter of the incident in the right-hand column that best matches each location in the left-hand column. (*2 points each*)

_____ 41. First Academy Building

_____ 42. a dining room in Vermont

_____ 43. a tree by the Devon River

_____ 44. a home in Boston

_____ 45. the Infirmary

_____ 46. the Butt Room

_____ 47. the Nagaumsett River

_____ 48. a dormitory room

_____ 49. the Far Common

_____ 50. the bank of the Nagaumsett

a. a "mock" trial was held

b. a confession occurred

c. a fight ended in it

d. Gene "became" Finny

e. a Carnival occurred

f. was occupied by troops

g. a "savage" was accused

h. site of a betrayal

i. a "psycho" testified

j. a conflict was resolved

Study Guide: A Separate Peace

Testing on the Novel

Critical Thinking and Writing

Directions: Write the answer to each of the following on a separate sheet of paper. (*20 points each*)

1. *A Separate Peace* has been classified by its author as an **allegory.** An allegory is a symbolic narrative in which fictional characters represent truths or generalizations about human existence. Discuss Phineas and Gene as **symbolic** or allegorical characters representing good and evil.

2. The physical **setting** of the novel is a prestigious boys' prep school, during World War II. Considering the development of the **plot,** discuss whether this story could occur elsewhere at some other time. Defend your reasoning.

3. At the end of Chapter 12, both Gene and the reader learn that Finny has died. Comment first on your reaction to this. Then discuss whether you believe Finny's death is ''necessary'' to the development of the **plot.** In other words, since the ''fates'' of a writer's characters are in his or her hands, why do you think Knowles thought Finny had to die?

4. The **plot** of a work presents a **conflict** (or conflicts) that leads to the **climax,** the point at which the conflict must be resolved or settled. Discuss the scene between Gene and Finny in the Infirmary, after Finny's second fall, as the climax, or turning point, of the novel.

5. *A Separate Peace* is about Gene Forrester's attempt, as a teenager, to establish his own values and his own identity and to mature into an adult. For whom, then, do you think Knowles wrote the novel? Is his message, or **theme,** intended exclusively for younger readers, or do you think he believed that others should read the novel as well? Defend your reasoning.

ANSWER KEY

Reading Guide Questions

Responding to the Novel

Analyzing the Novel

Answers to Identifying Facts questions may sometimes vary slightly. Answers to Interpreting Meanings and The Novel as a Whole questions, and *Writing About the Novel a*ssignments, will vary from those given in this Answer Key. ''Answers will vary'' responses should thus be used as guidelines only and not as model responses.

Chapter 1
Identifying Facts

1. Gene (the narrator) realizes that the marble stairs must be unusually hard.
2. It resembles the men, the giants of one's childhood, who years later are absolutely smaller and shrunken by age. The old giants have become pigmies.
3. Gene is thankful to have seen the tree because he realizes that nothing endures. He states that having seen the tree changes him.
4. The story flashes back to the summer of 1942 when the narrator and his friends are enrolled in the special summer session at Devon School.
5. Only Finny is eager to jump from the tree. The other four feel alarm and dread.
6. Gene and Finny are roommates and apparently friends as well.

Interpreting Meanings

7. Answers will vary. Students may cite any number of reasons for Gene's return to Devon, such as nostalgia or perhaps a class reunion. Museums typically house ''relics'' of previous times and are static in nature. Perhaps Gene wants his school to appear to be more dynamic, not something stale and old, because the school had seemed so vital during his years there.
8. Answers will vary. Students should mention most or all of the following points: The description implies places of dread, where something horrible had occurred. Gene mentions the hardness of the marble stairs and, of course, marble is slick and potentially dangerous. A tree is only fearful if it should fall on a person or if a person should fall

from it. Gene is anxious to see the fearful sites because he is curious about his own reactions to them. He wants to see whether he has changed.

9. Answers will vary. Students should mention most or all of the following points: Since the juniors, like Gene and Finny, are not yet old enough to be soldiers, the war may affect them in personal ways, such as loss of relatives or friends or loss of ''creature comforts.'' It may also affect their attitudes about life. The juniors also know that within a year, they will be the ones who are ''almost soldiers''; this is their last year of freedom.

10. Answers will vary. Students should mention most or all of the following points: The boys had heard that the seniors could jump from the tree, but that no upper Middler had tried. Finny had to take the challenge and, because of his nature, also had to get his group to try with him. Gene was the only other boy who jumped. Finny said that Gene was shamed into it, but Gene also did it so as not to lose face with Finny, the leader of the group. Being the only two to jump cemented the friendship, and the feelings of equality, between them. They became partners against the conformity demanded by the school, when Gene agrees to continue fooling around, instead of being on time for the dinner hour.

Chapter 2
Identifying Facts

1. Finny declares he will wear his pink shirt as an emblem of celebration of the bombing of Central Europe, since they don't have a flag to display proudly.

Study Guide: A Separate Peace

2. Gene is beginning to realize that Finny can get away with anything. He admits that he is envious but concludes that it's perfectly normal and there's no harm in envying one's best friend a little.

3. Finny wears the Devon School tie, explaining that the school is involved in everything that happens in the war and that Devon ought to be included.

4. Gene and Finny form the Super Suicide Society of the Summer Session.

5. Gene loses his balance and Finny grabs his arm. Gene later realizes he could have been killed and that Finny had "practically saved" his life.

Interpreting Meanings

6. Answers will vary. Perhaps Gene means that Finny's approach to life is one of pure acceptance of other people and pure joy in unconditional friendliness between people. Students may agree or disagree about this being a good "reason for living."

7. Answers will vary. Students should mention most or all of the following points: The faculty, like everyone else, found it difficult to be harsh with Finny. He was too charming and sincere to be taken as a threat. The "authority figures" might tend to be more lenient when there are more serious concerns, such as involvement in a world war, to occupy their thoughts. And it was summer session, a time traditionally more "free" at school, since the regular staff was on vacation. The instructors may also have seen their younger selves in the boys and not wanted to spoil these all too brief, carefree times.

8. Answers will be entirely subjective.

9. Answers will vary. Students should note that Gene has already said that it was a compliment to himself that such a unique person chose him as his best friend. Perhaps he feels that Finny is somehow his superior and that in order to maintain the balance of the friendship he has to defer to Finny's demands. Gene's reaction to "peer pressure" is fairly typical in that he does things he'd rather not in order to achieve some kind of acceptance.

Chapter 3
Identifying Facts

1. Gene and Finny open every meeting of the SSS of the SS by jumping from the tree themselves. Gene states it was one of the rules

Finny created without notice and that he hates it.

2. Finny invents "blitzball" because he is disgusted that badminton is considered a sport.

3. Finny makes Gene promise that he won't say anything to anyone about his breaking the swimming record.

4. Gene is shocked because it makes Finny seem too unusual for rivalry, and there were few relationships at Devon not based on rivalry.

5. Finny admits that Gene is his "best pal." Gene doesn't respond to this because something held him back from doing so.

Interpreting Meanings

6. Answers will vary. Students should note that Gene is obviously still trying to please Finny for some reason. He states that it never occurred to him to protest. Gene is afraid to risk confronting Finny about anything.

7. Answers will vary. Gene says he is glad, but more than likely his envy of Finny is increasing. Not only can Finny get away with everything, everyone likes him in spite of it.

8. Answers will vary. Perhaps the "truth" Gene is feeling is that Finny isn't really *his* best pal. Finny "calls all the shots" and Gene seems to be feeling a great deal of resentment. He may be feeling that he does all the giving in the relationship, that there isn't a balance of "give and take."

Chapter 4
Identifying Facts

1. Finny accuses Gene of striving to be head of their class.

2. Gene realizes that he and Finny would then be "even," that then they both would come out on top, Finny in athletics and Gene in academics.

3. Gene believes Finny is serious, in spite of his joking manner, and that Finny would be jealous of him becoming the head of the class.

4. Finally Gene concludes that he and Finny are even in "enmity"; that is, in their hatred of each other's accomplishments.

5. Gene then concludes that Finny has set out deliberately to prevent him from achieving his academic goal.

6. Gene states that he had always been a good student but that this knowledge about Finny caused him to become an exceptional one.

7. Gene continues to attend the meetings because he doesn't want Finny to "understand me as I understood him." In addition, Gene admits that he also didn't want Finny to excel him in jumping from the tree, even though that didn't matter.

8. Gene realizes that Finny had never been jealous of him even for a second, that there never was and never could have been any rivalry between them. Gene feels that Finny is truly a superior person to him, that Gene is not of the same quality as Finny.

9. Gene takes a step toward Finny, bends his knees, and jounces the limb.

10. For the first time, Gene jumps with sureness and completely without fear.

Interpreting Meanings

11. Answers will vary. Gene could have chosen to believe Finny was truly joking. Perhaps Gene chooses to "believe" Finny because he is feeling such jealously himself and needs to justify this.

12. Answers will vary. Students should mention most or all of the following points: Gene isn't being realistic. What he is failing to acknowledge is that he has allowed himself to be distracted by Finny's various diversions, for his own reasons, for his own need to have Finny's acceptance and approval. Gene's behavior is typical in that human beings very often look outside themselves for someone or something to blame for their behavior.

13. Answers will vary. There is no indication that Gene's act was premeditated. Just prior to the jump, Gene had admitted to himself that Finny had never been jealous of him, that Finny was a better person than he. Perhaps his action on the limb was some unconscious retaliation against Finny for being the better person. It is only after Gene hears Finny's body hit the bank that he jumps for the first time with sureness and without fear. It may be that Gene, who had only imagined that he and Finny were rivals, feels certain that no rivalry, imagined or real, can now occur.

Chapter 5
Identifying Facts

1. One of Finny's legs has been "shattered."
2. Gene feels that he "is" Phineas, to the life, including Finny's "optimistic awareness."

3. Dr. Stanpole tells Gene that Finny can never play sports again, that Finny must face that and accept it.

4. Finny apologizes to Gene for having had "a kind of feeling" about the accident that doesn't make any sense.

5. Dr. Stanpole comes in and then a nurse, and Gene is sent away. The next day the doctor decides Finny isn't well enough to have visitors and soon thereafter Finny is taken by ambulance to his home.

6. Finny denies Gene's confession and when Gene persists, Finny tells him to go away because Gene makes him sick.

7. Gene realizes he is injuring Finny again and that it might be an even deeper injury than the accident. Gene knows he must "take it back."

8. Gene promises himself he can make it all up to Finny at Devon.

Interpreting Meanings

9. Answers will vary. Perhaps Gene is suggesting that an accusation would have allowed him some relief from his feelings of guilt. As it is, he is the only one who knows what he did to Finny since Finny refuses to believe his confession. Gene is having to bear this burden entirely on his own. With an outside accusation, he might, he thinks, be able to concoct some defense, something he is unable to do in his isolated knowledge of the truth.

10. Answers will vary. Students should mention most or all of the following points: Gene thinks that if the situations were reversed, Finny would have told him the truth. Gene's guilt is becoming overwhelming and he needs release of some sort. He knows that Finny didn't deserve the kind of "punishment" Gene has inflicted upon him. Probably he needs to unburden himself. The old adage, "Confession is good for the soul," may be appropriate here. No doubt Gene will feel better than Finny, who will know for certain that the act was a treacherous one perpetrated by his "best pal."

11. Answers will vary. Students should note that Finny is a guileless, open, and trusting person. It probably is not within Finny's capability to believe that someone, particularly his best friend, would willfully wish him harm since he is incapable of such a notion himself. To have accepted Gene's "truth" would have been more than Finny could bear, since it would have negated what Gene calls one of Finny's "reasons for living," that is, the en-

joyment of "simple, unregulated friendliness" between people.

Chapter 6
Identifying Facts

1. Gene concludes that the point of the sermon was, "If you broke the rules, they broke you."
2. Gene hits Quackenbush because Quackenbush calls him "maimed."
3. Finny is relieved because, if Gene had taken another roommate, Finny would have been convinced that Gene was truly crazy. Finny admits he had had a trace of doubt since Gene had "talked so crazy" when he visited Finny at home.
4. Finny informs Gene that Gene is going to play sports for him since he can't any longer.
5. Gene feels he has lost part of himself to Finny, that all along he must have intended "to become a part of Phineas."

Interpreting Meanings

6. Answers will vary. Students should mention most or all of the following points: The summer had offered all of the boys at Devon a relatively carefree existence since rules had been relaxed considerably. It also had offered Gene, through his confusion about his relationship with Finny, a chance to gain self-knowledge that could have improved his own character. Instead, his awareness that Finny had never been jealous of him, for some reason, caused him to retaliate rather than to appreciate Finny as a unique and special friend.
7. Answers will vary. Students should note that Finny obviously, even though he can't openly admit his suspicions of Gene with regard to the accident, has doubts about Gene's friendship. He needs reassurance from Gene that his suspicions are totally unfounded.
8. Answers will vary. Perhaps, since Gene feels Finny is a superior person, he looks upon this as the only way he can hope to attain some of the basic goodness that he knows exists in Finny.

Chapter 7
Identifying Facts

1. Brinker accuses Gene of having "fixed it" so that Finny wouldn't be back in the fall and Gene could have their room to himself.

2. Gene manages to maintain control by treating the accusation as a joke, recounting a series of ridiculous "crimes" he had committed against Finny.
3. The one thing Gene couldn't say was that he had "pushed" Finny out of the tree.
4. Gene shifts attention from himself by making fun of one of the younger boys who wasn't particularly well accepted by the Butt Room crowd.
5. Leper, wearing long, wooden skis, goes in search of a beaver dam.
6. Gene is thrilled by Brinker's announcement, since it now enables him to consider the same possibility; to enlist and slam the door on the past, to break the pattern of his life. Gene decides that he will leave Devon and actively join the war effort.
7. Gene states that Finny's return caused all his thoughts of the day to fade "like that first false snowfall of the winter."

Interpreting Meanings

8. Answers will vary. Students should mention most or all of the following points: Right after the accident, Gene was hoping that someone would accuse him. Now that he is being accused he is unable to admit the truth even though he knows it might help to end his "living nightmare." To do so would prevent him from having the opportunity to try to make it all up to Finny upon his return to Devon. It would no longer be just *his* nightmare. To admit to "outsiders" what he had done would have forced Finny to accept the truth and would perhaps have ultimately ended their friendship.
9. Answers will vary. Students should mention most or all of the following points: Gene apparently is acknowledging that, unlike Finny who has the capacity for appreciation of life, he always has to find something negative in things, to make them less appealing than they were at first. Gene is perhaps obliquely admitting that he doesn't feel worthy of getting what he wants or loves. Or he may be acknowledging that he is only attracted to things and situations that contain a certain element of risk; that in this danger lies their appeal.
10. Answers will vary. Gene's differing conclusions may be simply a survival technique. As time passes and he gets further from the actual situation, perhaps his memory distorts the reality so that he can justify his current desire to "run away" from himself and make

a fresh start. Finny's absence also plays a big part in Gene's feelings about Devon.

Chapter 8
Identifying Facts

1. Gene feels a certain disapproval of Finny for complaining about a lost luxury (having no maids) since there is a war on.
2. Gene realizes that Finny needs him, that he wants Gene around in spite of everything.
3. Gene feels that peace has come back to Devon for him because Finny has returned and has chosen to show only Gene "the most humbling sides of his handicap."
4. Finny concludes there is no war, that it is a fake promoted entirely by fat old men to keep young people in their places.
5. Finny explains that he gets the "joke" about the war because he has suffered.
6. Gene and Finny are both startled by Finny's bitterness. Neither of them ever mentioned it and neither one ever forgot it was there.
7. Finny announces that he is going to coach Gene for the 1944 Olympics.
8. Finny tells Gene that up till then Gene had been lazy and hadn't known anything about himself.
9. Mr. Ludsbury tells Finny that all exercise must be aimed at the "approaching Waterloo," and entreats the boys to keep that in mind at all times. Finny's response is a simple, "No."

Interpreting Meanings

10. Answers will be entirely subjective.
11. Answers will vary. Perhaps Gene feels that he owes it to Finny, who needs him, to stay at Devon and fulfill his promise to himself that he will make it all up to Finny. Perhaps he also feels guilty that he could enlist and make a clean start but that Finny can't. Gene needs Finny as much as Finny needs Gene. Gene could never really have a fresh start without resolving the situation.
12. Answers will be entirely subjective.

Chapter Nine
Identifying Facts

1. Leper's enlistment makes Gene feel even more certain that the war is unreal.
2. Leper concludes that, "Everything has to evolve or else it perishes."

3. They all wonder whether they can measure up even to the minimum standard of the army, and they hope Leper is as heroic as they say he is.
4. Finny draws Gene into a world inhabited only by the two of them, with no war at all, training for the Olympics.
5. Gene convinces Brinker that they should do it for Finny who hasn't been involved in anything since his return to Devon. In addition, he and Brinker become co-conspirators when Brinker mentions there probably is a rule against such a carnival.
6. Finny opens the Games of the Winter Carnival by dousing a copy of the *Iliad* with cider and setting it afire.
7. Gene says Finny's "dance" was his "wildest demonstration of himself in the kind of world he loved; it was his choreography of peace."
8. Gene attributes his surpassing himself in the Decathlon, not to the cider but to their extraction, from the realities of life, of a "momentary, illusory, special and separate peace."
9. Gene receives an urgent telegram from Leper stating he has escaped and needs help.

Interpreting Meanings

10. Answers will vary. Students should note that the boys need something to make the notion of war less horrible. Since Gene and many of his classmates will likely be participating in the war before long, they need some sort of hope that it isn't as dreadful as they think. The images of war typically are not "clean." They are instead grim and terrifying, horrible and ugly.
11. Answers will vary. Students should note that Gene is no doubt wondering whether they will evolve sufficiently or whether they will perish.
12. Answers will vary. Students should note that the only real interaction between Leper and any of the boys at Devon has been with Gene. When Leper returned from his search for the beaver dam, Gene "protected" him from Brinker's ridicule. In his time of need, it is logical that Leper would turn to someone who apparently accepted him.

Chapter 10
Identifying Facts

1. The narrator reveals that he never got to the war. That he entered the army as the war

was winding down, and his time was spent in shuttling around the country, being trained in weapons that quickly became obsolete.

2. Gene concludes that, since one doesn't "escape" from the army, Leper must have escaped from the enemies within the country, that is, spies.

3. Gene reacts with fear because he reasons that if Leper is psycho, the army has done it to him, and that he and his classmates, who "were on the brink of the army," might be the next victims.

4. Leper supports his charge that Gene is a "savage underneath" by citing "the time you knocked Finny out of the tree," that "time you crippled him for life."

5. Gene admits that he was too ashamed of himself to leave and that sometimes one needs to know the facts too much to leave.

6. Leper says the army may be psycho because "they turned everything inside out."

7. Gene screams at Leper to "Shut up" and he runs back to town, leaving Leper alone.

8. Gene says he doesn't care about what happened to Leper because it had nothing to do with him, that he didn't ever want to hear any more of it.

Interpreting Meanings

9. Answers will vary. Perhaps Gene is caught up in the notion that certain aspects of war are "glamorous" and "exciting," such as being involved with spies. He doesn't want to accept the fact that Leper didn't meet up with "a clean image of war."

10. Answers will be entirely subjective.

11. Answers will vary. Probably Gene reacts so violently to Leper's story because it terrifies him. He doesn't know how to deal with such an outpouring. Contrary to what he says, he does care. And he realizes that it does have something to do with him: that the war could drive anyone crazy, and that Leper needs help that Gene is unable to give.

Chapter 11
Identifying Facts

1. Gene wants only to see Finny because, "With him there was no conflict except between athletes," that conflict "in which victory would go to whoever was the strongest in body and heart."

2. During the snowball fight, Finny betrays his original teammates and confuses loyalties. He ends up being the target for everyone.

3. Brinker, who had discerned the truth about Leper for himself, is bewildered. He is also annoyed that anyone had let Leper enlist, and sympathetic.

4. Brinker says Gene has put off enlisting because he pities Finny. Brinker says Finny should be kidded about being "crippled" so that he will begin to accept it.

5. Brinker states firmly that everything about Finny's accident should be "cleared up and forgotten."

6. Finny states that his having seen Leper for himself convinced him there was a "real war on."

7. Gene thinks the seniors are plotting some kind of prank before they leave Devon.

8. Brinker announces they are gathered to investigate Finny's accident.

9. Gene calculates that Leper is no threat, that no one will believe him since he is "deranged" and people in that condition can't testify.

10. Finny states that he doesn't care and, in tears, he screams at Brinker to get the rest of the facts.

11. The final sound the boys hear is Finny falling down the white marble stairs.

Interpreting Meanings

12. Answers will vary. Students should note that Finny holds the schoolboy ethic of not being gullible, especially to authority, but he follows his own rules, one of which is loyalty to his best friend.

13. Answers will vary. Students should note that ever since Gene had backed out of enlisting with him, Brinker had decided to be as military as possible, short of joining up. He seemed to feel it was his duty to account for the two "casualties" in their class.

14. Answers will vary. Perhaps Finny really doesn't care. Maybe he just wants the matter to be forgotten. Since he apparently has been able to accept Gene's behavior, perhaps he resents the interference of Brinker and the others. Finny may have mentioned that Leper was available to "testify," hoping that he would corroborate Finny's "memory" of the occurrence.

Chapter 12

Identifying Facts

1. Gene is afraid that Finny will curse him, lose his head completely, and maybe be worse off for it.

2. Gene reasons that Finny didn't mind Gene's helping him because Finny had thought of Gene as an extension of himself.

3. Dr. Stanpole states that Finny has broken his leg again but that it's a cleaner break, a simple fracture.

4. Finny accuses Gene of coming to break something else in him.

5. Finny admits he has been writing letters all winter trying to get some service to accept him. The result has been that none will accept him because of his medical report.

6. Gene tells Finny he wouldn't be any good in the war even if nothing had happened to his leg.

7. Gene tells Finny that what he had done in the tree was because of "some ignorance inside me, some crazy thing inside me, something blind." Finny tells Gene that he understands and that he believes Gene.

8. Dr. Stanpole concludes that some of the bone marrow must have escaped into the bloodstream, gone directly to his heart, and stopped it.

9. Gene says he never cried about Finny because he had a feeling Finny's funeral was his own and one doesn't cry in such a case.

Interpreting Meanings

10. Answers will vary. Students should note that the scene of Finny being carried out in the chair reminded Gene of how Finny was always the one to do the carrying, before. Gene reflects on Finny's nobility of character.

11. Answers will vary. Gene probably at least thinks he is telling Finny the truth. Since Gene had determined there was no rivalry between them, that he had imagined it all, he had no logical or rational reason for wanting to hurt Finny. Perhaps it was, after all, some ignorance inside him that he had no knowledge of and, consequently, no control over.

12. Answers will vary. Gene may mean that his emotions died along with Finny.

Chapter 13

Identifying Facts

1. The Army Air Force Parachute Riggers' School occupies the Far Commons, bringing their sewing machines with them.

2. Gene concludes no one ever accused him of Finny's death either because they couldn't believe it or because they couldn't understand it.

3. Brinker's father tells them that it's important to do the right thing for the long run, not just for the moment. He is concerned that the boys are more interested in comfort than in seeing lots of action.

4. Gene concludes that wars are a result, not of "generations and their special stupidities," but are "made instead of something ignorant in the human heart."

5. Phineas alone had escaped being "pitted violently against something in the world" around him and, consequently, he had escaped having the "simplicity and unity" of his character broken. Gene says that, since nothing in Finny's world "had broken his harmonious and natural unity," he, Gene, finally had.

6. Gene states that his fury was gone because "Phineas had absorbed it and taken it with him, and I was rid of it forever."

7. Gene says his war ended before he ever put on a uniform because he had been on active duty at Devon and had killed his enemy there.

8. People who "sight" the enemy begin "an obsessive labor or defense," begin "to parry the menace they saw facing them by developing a particular frame of mind."

9. Everyone except Finny constructed lines against the enemies they thought they saw, at infinite cost to themselves. Gene wonders if "this enemy" ever attacked at all and if indeed he was "the enemy."

Interpreting Meanings

10. Answers will be entirely subjective.

11. Answers will vary. Students should note that Gene is talking about all the conflicts within human nature. Man does not seem to be basically peaceful, as evidenced in Gene's relationships with Finny, Leper, and Brinker, for example.

12. Answers will vary. Perhaps Gene means that the best way, if there is a best way, to enter a war is to do so without hatred. Gene states earlier that he believes wars are a result of "something ignorant in the human heart."

Maybe Gene means he has conquered the ''ignorance,'' the hatred, in his own heart and can, therefore, join the war feeling that he won't be adding to the world's ignorance.

13. Answers will vary. Students should note that Gene concludes that ''enemies'' exist only in our minds because we create them. Somehow we determine that these ''enemies'' are a threat to us and we go on the defensive. We plan our attack, determined to rid ourselves of this threat. Gene may be suggesting that he attacked an ''enemy'' (Finny) who never considered Gene a threat, who never attacked him back, who, in reality, was never an enemy at all, and the cost to Gene was infinite.

The Novel as a Whole

1. Answers will vary. Students should note that Gene Forrester is the protagonist of the novel since the story is primarily about his experiences, observations, and conclusions. Further, the story is told by him as a first-person narrator.

2. Answers will vary. Students should mention most or all of the following points: Finny is Gene's antagonist, his adversary, but only because Gene imagines that he is. The confusion Gene feels about Finny's function in his life leads him to feel that Finny is his enemy. Acting on that false assumption, Gene goes through a series of reactions. Finally, even though he concludes that he was wrong about the rivalry he suspected between himself and Finny, Gene's ''savage'' nature causes him to act against his ''imagined'' enemy. Subsequently, then, since Gene has to deal with trying to rectify his action, he becomes his own adversary, his own antagonist. Other antagonists are Leper, whose army experiences Gene doesn't want to hear about or deal with, and Brinker, who determines that Finny's accident must be investigated. In addition, the war itself is an adversary since it opposes the ordered and logical existence so important to Gene.

3. Answers will vary. Students should mention most or all of the following points: With regard to Gene, Leper causes him to face his ''savage'' self by openly confronting Gene about causing Finny's accident. He also causes Gene to acknowledge his fear about the war and what it might do to him personally. Leper causes Finny to finally accept the reality of war, and his big impact on Finny results from his ''testifying'' at the investigation. His testimony, although he stops short of naming Gene as the one who jounced the limb, causes Finny to accept the truth about Gene—that the one person in whom he had placed his trust cannot be trusted. Therefore, Leper, in essence, causes both boys to face realities they were attempting to avoid.

4. Answers will vary. Students should mention most or all of the following points: Mr. Hadley's function in the novel is to serve as a foil to his son Brinker. The author uses him to show contrasting opinions about the ''glory'' of war. Mr. Hadley tells Gene and Brinker that they should strive to achieve the best military record possible since to serve one's country is one's greatest moment and greatest privilege. Brinker, who had been the first to say he would enlist, resentfully concludes that people like his father are responsible for the war that he and other young men will have to fight.

5. Answers will vary. Students should mention most or all of the following points: Based on the reader's knowledge that Gene realized, just before he caused Finny's accident, that Finny was not his enemy, it is unlikely that the act was premeditated. His anger at himself, and his anger at this further revelation of Finny's perfection lashed out. Further, Gene admits to Finny that it was ''something blind'' in him which caused him to act, some ignorance of that savage part of himself. As far as the reader can tell, Gene apparently didn't conceive of a deliberate plan to hurt Finny. His action was obviously an impulsive one.

6. Answers will vary. Students should mention most or all of the following points: Gene tries to ignore the war but finally, facing the reality of it, accepts his duty and joins the Navy, knowing that he can do so without contributing any hatred to it. Finny pretends there is no war. Finally he admits to Gene that this was simply a ''front,'' and that he had been trying all winter long to get accepted into some branch of service. Leper, of course, becomes a ''casualty,'' forced to escape from the army because he cannot cope with what is happening to him. Brinker also accepts his duty and joins the Coast Guard, but he does so with a changed perspective. He is not, as he once thought he was, eager to ''serve.''

7. Answers will vary. Students should mention most or all of the following points: The novel is set in New Hampshire at Devon School.

The action is closely bound in with the New England seasons and the school buildings and grounds. The dual nature of the school, and its inhabitants, helps set the tone of the story. The two "fearful sites" directly affect the development of the plot. The other setting element that is a main component in creating the atmosphere from which the story evolves is the historic time of the novel, 1942 and 1943. Since World War II is being fought, this affects not only the perspective and behavior of Gene but all the students and faculty at Devon as well.

8. Answers will vary. For some possible interpretations, see "Symbolism," in *Elements of the Novel.*

9. Answers will vary. For a discussion of *theme,* see "The Themes of *A Separate Peace,*" in *Elements of the Novel.*

Writing About the Novel

A Creative Response

1. Answers will vary, but should indicate that students understand the relationship between Gene and Finny right before Finny's death.

2. Answers will vary, but should indicate that students understand Finny's background and character.

3. Answers will vary, but should indicate that students understand how Gene's feelings about Finny must have evolved over the years.

A Critical Response

4. Answers will vary. However, whichever position the student takes, he/she should include specific references to Finny's character as developed by the author and address Finny's character as an allegorical symbol.

5. Answers will vary. However, whichever position students take, they should support their opinions by using specific references to the novel.

6. Answers will vary. Students should mention most or all of the following points: Leper and Brinker are, much like Gene and Finny, opposites. Leper functions in a world of his own, spending his time and energy being, as Brinker disparagingly labels him, a "naturalist." The mysteries of the natural world are what matter to Leper. When he becomes involved in a part of the "man-made" world, as a soldier in the army, he can no longer function and has a nervous breakdown.

Brinker, on the other hand, as the class leader, is strongly affected by "reality." He feels a responsibility to ensure that he and his classmates "do things right." Brinker is the first to talk about enlisting, although, ironically, Leper is the first to enlist. After learning of Leper's nervous breakdown, Brinker focuses his feeling of responsibility for "the class" on clearing up the matter of Finny's accident, so that there will be no more casualties than are necessary.

7. Answers will vary. Students should mention most or all of the following points: Mr. Prud'homme and Mr. Ludsbury function only to the extent that they represent the immediate "adult" world of the Devon students. As a teacher in the special Summer Session, Mr. Prud'homme relaxes the "standards" of the school, allowing the boys a peaceful, "gypsy" summer. When the regular term begins, however, Mr. Ludsbury insists on proper behavior, that is, conformity to "regimentation."

8. Answers will vary. Students should mention most or all of the following points: The novel is indeed a linear narrative. Except for the beginning and ending of the novel, and the trip to Leper's home in Vermont, told from Gene's perspective as an adult, the action of the story is chronological. As Gene relates the events of the special Summer Session, the novel at first concentrates only on the relationship between him and Finny. Eventually, however, Knowles brings both Brinker and Leper into the story of Gene and Finny, with Brinker's decision to investigate Finny's accident and Leper's testimony at the "trial."

9. Answers will vary. Students should mention most or all of the following points. The main images of the seasons must be included (i.e., the bare trees and snowfalls of winter; Finny after the accident; the peaceful sights and sounds of summer; the first days of friendship, etc.). The metaphor of the tree ("an irate, steely black steeple"), personification ("the playing fields were optimistically green and empty before us. . .") and simile ("The leg in its cast was like a sea anchor dragged behind") are just a few of the many examples of figures of speech used throughout the novel.

Going Beyond the Novel

A Creative Response

Responses to Creative Response assignments will vary greatly.

Study Guide: A Separate Peace

Responses to Critical Response assignments will vary greatly.

Testing on the Novel

Developing Vocabulary

A.
1. b	2. e	3. n	4. m	5. a
6. o	7. k	8. i	9. j	10. g
11. h	12. c	13. d	14. l	15. f
16. q	17. t	18. s	19. r	20. p

B.
1. j	2. c	3. n	4. b	5. d
6. k	7. o	8. f	9. m	10. g
11. a	12. h	13. l	14. e	15. i
16. t	17. p	18. s	19. r	20. q

C.
1. a	2. b	3. b	4. d	5. c
6. a	7. d	8. c	9. a	10. c
11. a	12. d	13. b	14. c	15. b
16. a	17. a	18. a	19. d	20. b
21. b	22. d	23. c	24. c	25. a

Understanding What Happened/ Recognizing Elements of the Novel

A.
1. T	2. F	3. T	4. F	5. T
6. F	7. F	8. F	9. T	10. T
11. T	12. T	13. T	14. T	15. F
16. F	17. T	18. T	19. F	20. F
21. T	22. F	23. F	24. F	25. F
26. F	27. T	28. F	29. T	30. T

B.
31. i	32. d	33. g	34. e	35. h
36. c	37. j	38. f	39. b	40. a

C.
41. i	42. g	43. h	44. b	45. j
46. a	47. c	48. d	49. f	50. e

Critical Thinking and Writing

1. Answers will vary. Students should mention most or all of the following points: Knowles portrays Phineas as the embodiment of the "ideal" human being, one who does not need to "sight enemies" or to belittle others in order to justify his own existence. Therefore, Phineas represents the "good" in mankind, the accepting, generous, guileless human being. Gene, of course, through his attempt to "destroy" the ideal (Finny) that he couldn't achieve, symbolically represents the "evil," or savage, side of mankind, the critical, selfish, insecure human being.

2. Answers will vary. Students should mention most or all of the following points: Because the story centers on the attempt of Gene Forrester to establish his own identity, the setting of the novel, with regard to both place and time, could be different and still allow for the journey into himself that Gene takes. That the story occurs during the time of World War II certainly adds to the plot development, by increasing the tension that teenagers already feel in their efforts to mature. However, because Knowles's purpose was to depict the "darker streaks of human nature," he could have done so without this added dimension. Knowles, of course, extends his message and makes it universal, rather than limiting it to the individual, by having Gene recognize that his own "ignorance in the human heart" exists on a world-wide scale. (See "Setting" under *Elements of the Novel* for a reply to the contrary.)

3. Reactions will vary. However, since Knowles uses Finny as the individual "victim" of man's darker nature, it is logical that he makes the most of this character's function by having him die. In addition, since Finny is the embodiment of a free-spirit, one who lives life to the utmost, his actual physical death is consistent with the "death" of that spirit, resulting from his physical crippling and from his realization that the one person in the world he had trusted had betrayed him. As a Christ-like symbol, he dies as a savior, in order to make Gene whole.

4. Answers will vary. Students should mention most or all of the following points: The scene between Gene and Finny in the Infirmary finally resolves the conflict between them— Gene confesses and Finny not only faces the truth, that Gene had betrayed him, but also forgives Gene. The tension between the two characters, that had existed throughout the novel, is finally eased and, in time, Gene is also able to face the "truth" about himself and conquer his "savage" side.

5. Answers will vary. However, since Knowles's style of writing is sophisticated and since he extends his "message" to a universal level, connecting Gene's discovery about himself to his belief that wars result from "something blind" in human beings, Knowles obviously wrote his book for a wide range of readers.

For Further Reading

Other Works by the Author

Morning in Antibes (1962)
Double Vision: American Thoughts Abroad (travel) (1964)
Indian Summer (1966)
Phineas (short stories) (1968)
The Paragon (1971)
Spreading Fires (1974)
A Vein of Riches (1978)
Peace Breaks Out (1981)
A Stolen Past (1983)
The Private Life of Axie Reed (1986)

More About the Author

Periodicals:

Book Week, July 24, 1966
Commonweal, December 9, 1960
Contemporary Literary Criticism, Volume I, 1973; Volume IV, 1975
Esquire, March 1985
Harper's, July 1966
Life, August 5, 1966
Manchester Guardian, May 1, 1959
New Statesman, May 2, 1959
New York Times Book Review, February 7, 1960; August 14, 1966
Saturday Review, August 13, 1966
Times Literary Supplement, May 1, 1959

Related Works

Cormier, Robert, *The Chocolate War*
Golding, William, *Lord of the Flies*
Salinger, J. D., *The Catcher in the Rye*

NOTES

NOTES

NOTES

NOTES

NOTES

NOTES

NOTES

NOTES